AF600782

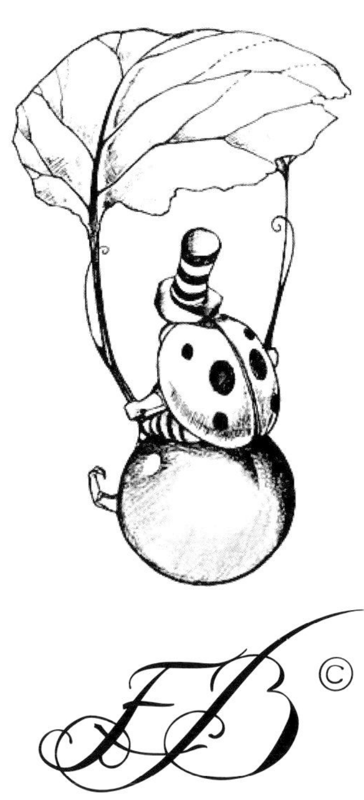

The Fantastic World Of
Claus Brusen

Ole Lindboe

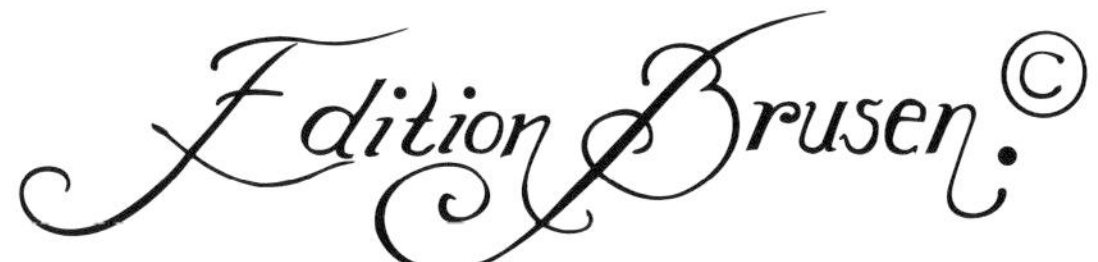

First Edition 2006

Colophon

The Fantastic World of Claus Brusen

First Edition

Bibliography
A. Alvarez: Natten, Tiderne Skifter 1995.
André Breton: De surrealistiske manifester. Gyldendal 1972.
Jakob Levinsen: Helte og Hobitter. Lindhardt & Ringhof 2004.
Ole Lindboe & Sven Kreiner Møller (Red.): Virkelige Eventyr, Spar Knægt 19
Tzvetan Todorov: Den fantastiske litteratur. Klim 1989.

Photography: Hans Nielsen og Claus Brusen
Translation: Geoffrey Reynolds
Graphic Design: Marcel Salome Re-Art
Printed by Re-Art & Mercurius, The Netherlands
www.re-art.com

ISBN: 87-990636-1-1

www.clausbrusen.com

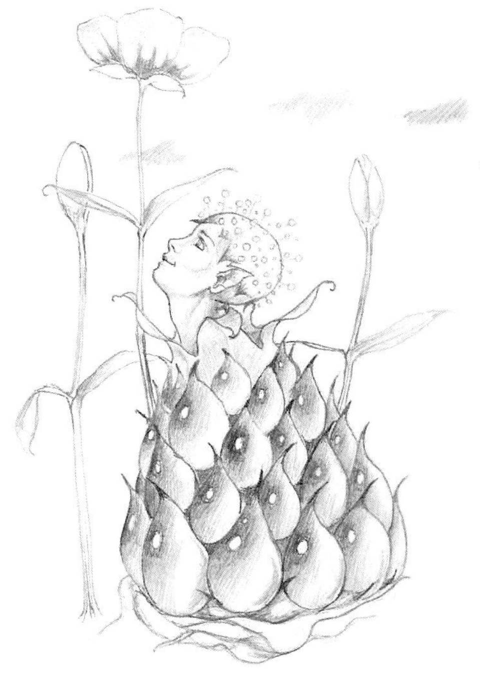

Nactalius is the name of a wondrous fairy tale world created by the painter Claus Brusen. The artist is a profoundly original painter that through his pictures leads us into a universe of apparent innocence. But there is more going on than meets the eye. To enter Nactalius is like buying a ticket to an enigmatic world harboring its own distinctive dramas.

The book about Claus Brusen and his fantastic world is written by Ole Lindboe, editor of Magasinet Kunst (The Art Magazine) and author of a long series of art books.

Introduction

by

Patrick Woodroffe

This artist does live in reality, but he also governs a very pretty world of his own, a planet where he can invent whatever he desires within seconds, his new territory costing him just some careful real work but no real money. I feel sure that most fantasy artists feel utterly imprisoned in their real world, but they can gain utter freedom on their own planet, a kingdom where they can even make the sun come up whenever they like, even in the middle of the night. All the colours are in control. Grey can be replaced by bright orange.

Claus has a rather unusual system for painting. Most artists that I know paint on a white background, but Claus begins his own world with dark black, a sad background for pictures that become happier within seconds. In fact his world never looks sad. We see no violence, no threats of war, not even a tiny family argument. We never even see an animal yearning to eat another. The restaurant menu seems to have only strawberries on the list, certainly no red blood to drink.

The directions to which the characters look must also have some relevance. It seems to be always to the left. Claus has always been in love with innocent little animals, not just butterflies, but also some beetles from Liverpool, so I feel sure that England fits in very well with his own world.

Claus is also unusual in another way. Many artists I know, especially myself, are obsessed with their own work, but Claus has already worked for the benefit of other painters. He has made not just an enormous collection of other artists´ paintings - he has already organized an exhibition and published a book. We are now working together on a project that I feel sure shall become very important - the idea to set up a global club of fantasy art, friendship between as many artists as possible, the target being to encourage their confidence and success. The latest idea for the title is "UN-ART" – UNITED NATIONS in encouragement of 21st. century fantasy ART - to help the real world to become almost as much in charge as the artists´ own worlds – global peace, global friendship, GLOBAL BLISS!

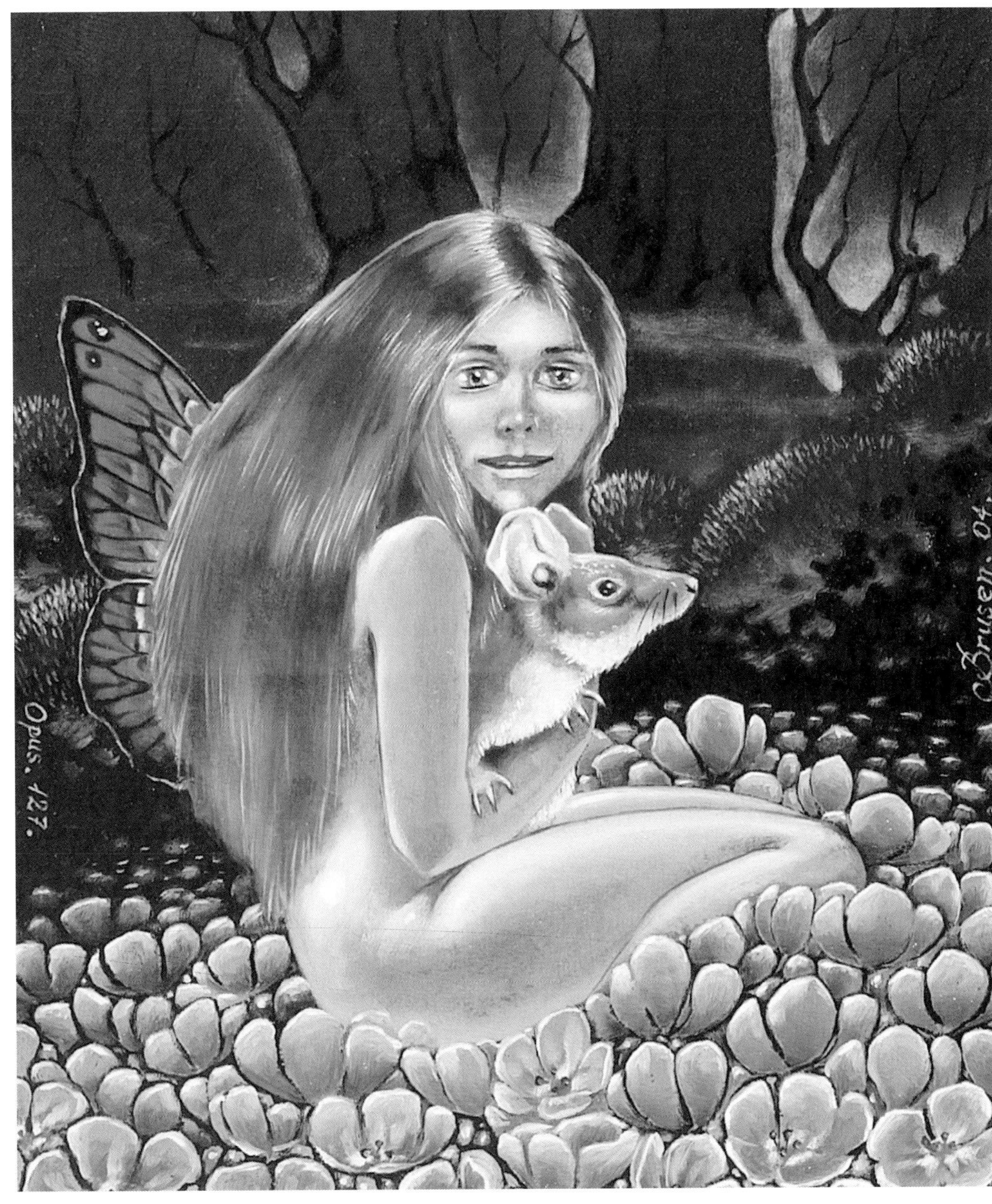

Opus 127
Woodroffe Fairy
Oil on Panel
size 15 x 12 cm
2004

Inspired by the females in Patricks paintings

Index

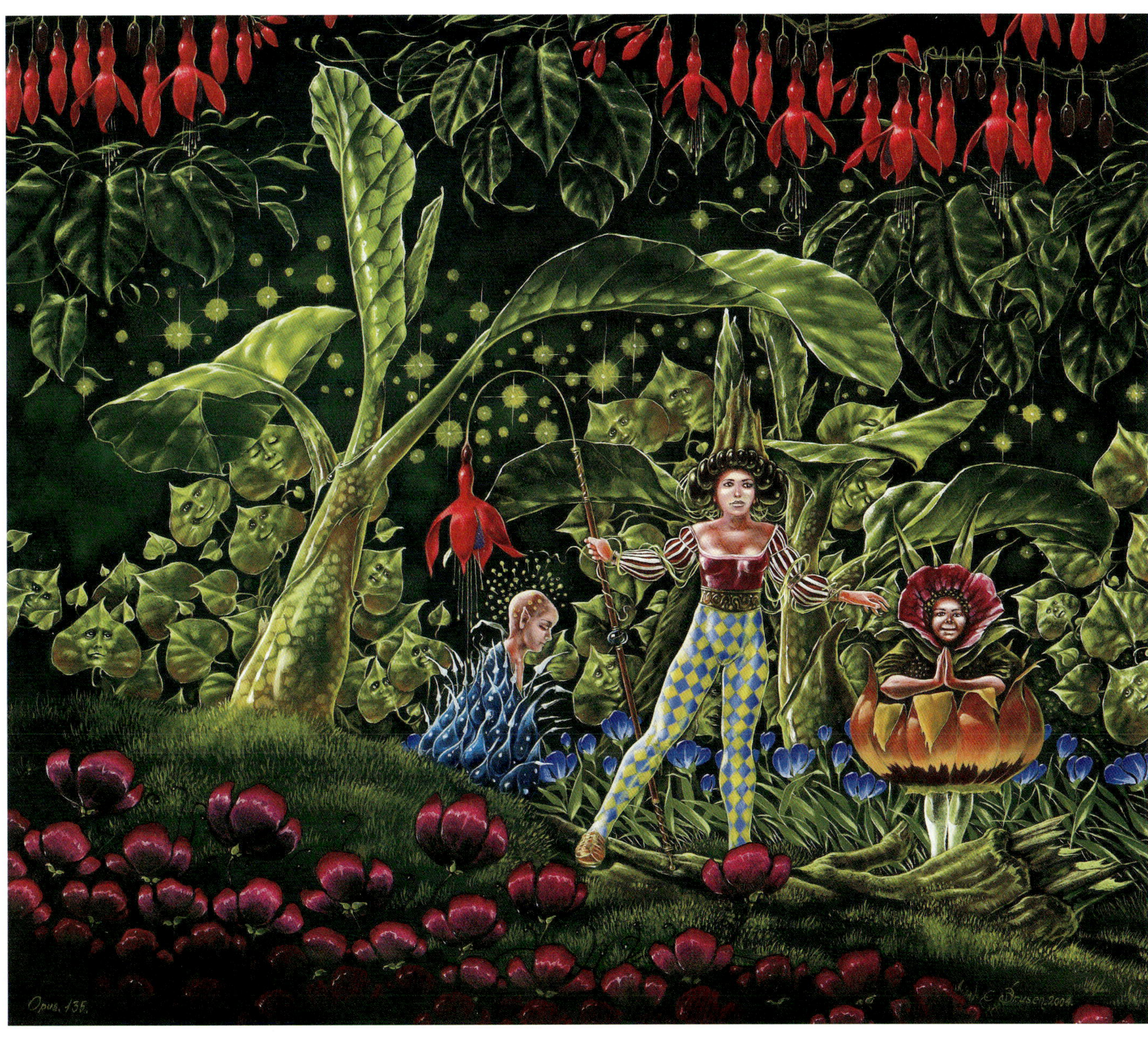

Opus 135
The Garden of Unearthly Delight
Oil on Panel
size 37 x 42 cm
2004

The Fantastic World Of

Claus Brusen

by

Ole Lindboe

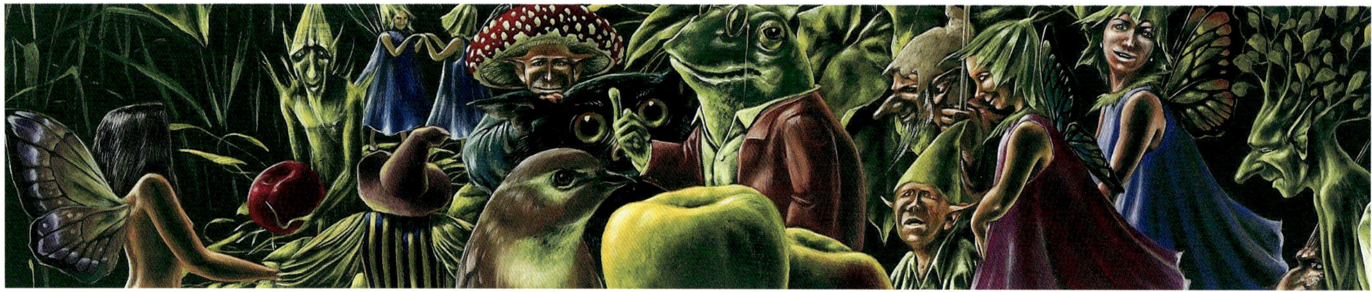

Once upon a time in Nactalius

We find ourselves in a forest. It is dense and green and lush. Small delicate flowers grow from the forest floor. A bird flies through the air, flapping rapidly. Everything seems normal – or does it?

Because standing in one corner of the forest is a little naked elven girl on the lookout. There in the back of a glade two similar naked elves can be seen, maybe busy discussing something. In the middle of the glade, in the center of it all, is a little manikin wearing a toadstool-like head covering. He looks cheerfully conspiratorial out towards the viewer while leaning against a menhir. Several other small creatures appear in the forest.

In another corner of the glade we see a diminutive dwarfish person who is peacefully sitting amidst the greenery engaged in gazing at the two naked elven girls. And up in the trees two small elf-like male creatures swing through the leaves.

The whole scene as we see it in a painting by Claus Brusen is imbued with an atmosphere of purity and innocence. And yet: On closer inspection everything is not pure innocence. Because the naked elven girls are not quite so innocent as first assumed. After all, they are naked, and the consciousness of sin entered the world along with nakedness, as we remember from the Bible.

The erotic is not just a beautiful fairy tale. It can be synonymous with perdition and eternal damnation.

And then there are the beautiful elves. Are they only good? Nay, from other fairy tales we know that they are full of contradictions. They can be deceitful. They can entice people, lead them deep into the forest and get them to lose their senses so they never come out again. The same holds true for dwarves. They are not just straightforward, simple and loyal. They can be extremely stubborn, even spiteful.

It is only in the sentimental versions of fairy tales that all ends well and the good are only good and the evil are only evil. Throughout history many of the old fairy tales have been altered, as was the case with the Brothers Grimm fairy tales in Denmark, which were first translated by Carl Ewald in 1905. The tales were filled with too much pleasantness, while the original versions were much more ribald and full of cruelty, hate, love and other risqué activities.

In the real fairy tales things are considerably more ambiguous. Powers of darkness and light actually do battle with each other. Black magic and white magic are put to use but you can't always tell which is which. There is an abundance of disguises in the world of magic. Nothing is what it appears to be.

And that's also how it is in the world of artist Claus Brusen. He calls it Nactalius. It is fabulous, it certainly is. But the fantastical has many adventures in store for us once we enter the story. Everything seems endlessly naïve, at least on the surface. But do we dare believe it? Hardly.

When the fairy tale found Claus Brusen or Claus Brusen found the fairy tail isn't really to say. It must be an infection that slowly developed through childhood and youth to break out in adulthood.

In reality his career as an artist is short. He made his debut in 1983, but it wasn't until 2001 that he had his first actual gallery debut. Since then it's gone like wildfire. And already today he's on his way to an international career.

Now that is a fairy tale.

Claus Brusen's world is a universe of the authentic and the imaginary. What's unique is that we never quite know when the one ends and the other begins.

The strange appears side by side with the sinister and the marvelous. The harmless and the threatening appear side by side. Now be sure not to take any of it at face value.

New adventurers can start her.

If they dare.

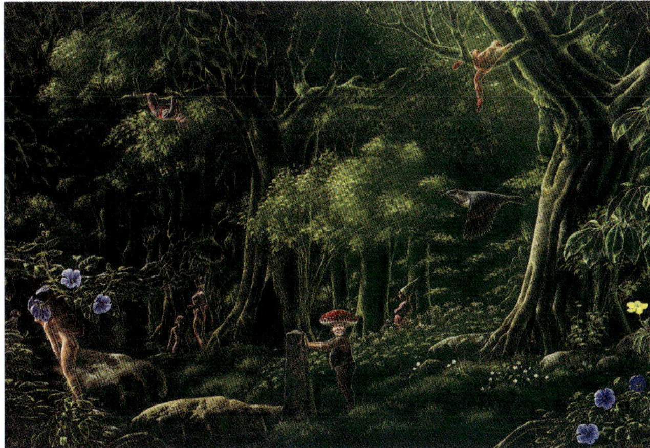

Opus 6
Forest Playground
Oil on Panel
size 40 x 60 cm
2000

Chapter 1

Once long ago

Once upon a time. That's how fairy tales began way back when there were real fairy tales. But the time for great tales is apparently over. The world has become so atomized, so splintered that we cannot cope with understanding it as a whole, maybe because there is no whole anymore. That's how it was set forth in the political world approaching the recent millennium.

So it seems we have also become so rational, so well informed, that the irrational has been banished to go stand in the corner of superstition. It isn't politically correct to believe in fairy tales or the fantastic at all. Those things are, at best, relegated to childhood. Children and the young at heart can go ahead and devote their time to fairy tales, but for "real adults" it is only harmless entertainment. Or is it?

Cynical reason has taken over reality and the world, so shouldn't one really think that there was even a bigger need for fairy tales than ever?

Surrealism's century

In the world of pictorial art surrealism, for many years, represented the most exaggerated fantasy. For this very reason it was severely denounced and criticized. Until the genre was suddenly favourably embraced and perhaps ended by being harmless.

Surrealism flourished in the 1920's. The first surrealist manifesto was published in 1924 and the penman was the writer André Breton. And he began his manifesto by writing: "So strong is the belief in life, in what is most fragile in life, real life. I mean – that in the end this belief is lost. Man, that inveterate dreamer....". And Breton concerns himself with the daily grind that most people's lives become, and he praises hallucinations and illusions that he calls " a not insignificant source of trifling pleasure".

Breton goes on to warn us most emphatically against the clarity of reason: "clarity bordering on stupidity, a dog's life!" And he concludes: "It is not the fear of madness that will oblige us to leave the flag of imagination furled...".

The surrealists offended many art lovers (and the bourgeoisie) by concerning themselves with a number of taboos such as the sexual, the violent, the forbidden, the horrifying and the disgusting.

The reality of dreams

From the start surrealism was preoccupied with psychoanalysis that had recently shed light on the many repressions that most people are filled with. Repressions that often pop up in our dreams and often symbolically disguised.

Together with the other surrealists, Sigmund Freud, the father of psychoanalysis, and his thoughts about dreams and the unconscious, fascinated André Breton. Breton wrote: "Freud very rightly brought his critical faculties to bear upon the dream. It is, in fact, inadmissible that this considerable portion of psychic activity (since, at least from man's birth until his death, thought offers no solution of continuity, the sum of the moments of the dream, from the point of view of time, and taking into consideration only the time of pure dreaming, that is the dreams of sleep, is not inferior to the sum of the moments of reality, or, to be more precisely limiting, the moments of waking) has still today been so grossly neglected......Thus the dream finds itself reduced to a mere parenthesis, as is the night."

The great surrealists

The first surrealists arrived on the scene under the motto "Nothing but the marvelous is beautiful". Max Ernst (1891-1976), Salvador Dali (1904-1989), Rene Magritte (1898-1967), Joan Miró (1893-1983) and the photographer Man Ray (1890-1977) were a few who led the way in a movement that would come to cast long shadows over art right up to today.

In Denmark it was first and foremost Vilhelm Freddie (1909-1996) who set surrealism's agenda. But after the first scare had abated, it was as though surrealism ran out of steam. Perhaps because so much else was going on in the world of art in these years.

In the 1960's and 70's a variant of surrealism made its appearance, so-called magic realism, which built upon some of the same ideas as surrealism. In Denmark this movement was represented by a group of painters and graphic artists who were associated with Gallery Passepartout in the center of Copenhagen. These artists included Jørgen Boberg, Lars Rasmussen, Claus Bojesen, Ole Ahlberg, Hans Henrik Lerfeldt and others. They wanted imagination and the mythological back in art again. But they were quickly driven out on a sidetrack by the official art world. Suddenly it was Fluxus and Eks-school (the experimental school) and other avant-garde movements that took over.

Regardless, throughout the 1970's and afterwards, Denmark could muster a long line of fine surrealistic painters: Thor Lindeneg, Hakon Nyström, Bente Olesen Nyström, Ingvad Holmefjord, Finn Mickelborg and outsiders like Carsten Svennson, Stig Weye and Poul Anker Bech. And way out on the edge, the overlooked – and profoundly peculiar – painter Otto Frello.

The literature of fantasy

But it wasn't only in the pictorial arts that the remarkable was blossoming. Surrealism had a literary start and throughout the history of literature there are several examples of authors who cultivated the fantastical. Especially names like H.P. Lovecraft, C.S. Lewis and Lewis Caroll ("Alice in Wonderland") have become beacons for the flourishing that fantastical literature has experienced in recent times. But also writers like Jonathan Swift ("Gulliver's Travels"), A.A. Milne ("Winnie the Pooh"), and Kenneth Graham ("The Wind in the Willows"), as different as they may be – belong to the fantastical genre.

Men of letters, and others, are bewildered as to how to define the genre. The author Tzvetan Todorov attempts the difficult task in his classical work "The Fantastic Literature": "There are fairy tales that contain elements of the supernatural without the reader ever doubting their nature, for he knows that it shouldn't be taken literally. When animals speak, we don't concern ourselves, because we realize the words of the text have another meaning, specifically, the allegorical.

Lovecraft, who was known around the world for his gothic horror novels imbued with the supernatural, played the provocateur: "A tale is fantastic if the reader experiences a feeling of profound fear and dread, sensing the presence of undreamt of worlds and powers."

The lord of the rings

The English Oxford professor and author, J.R.R. Tolkien, more than almost anyone else, became a significant person for the genre of fantasy – in both literature and the pictorial arts. He released "The Hobbit" in 1937, the precursor for the trilogy "The Lord of the Rings" which was first published in 1954.

The fairy tale about the magic ring was originally told to his children, but he eventually decided to write it down. He developed this universe with inspiration from ancient myths, the Icelandic Sagas, etc. In "The Silmarillion" we can read about the greater context in which his fairy tale takes place. The most incredible about Tolkien is his ability to create an utterly unique universe where the good do battle against the evil and where it's teeming with detailed descriptions, cunning minor characters, trolls, dragons, elves and other supernatural creatures. Tolkien has been a cult phenomenon for a long time, also for "fantastic painters" throughout the world. It can be said that all the attention focused on Tolkien has created an atmosphere for an increasing interest in the fabulous and the fantastic. "The Fellowship of the Ring" clearly plays an important inspirational roll to a painter such as Claus Brusen. Nactalius is a universe that is unmistakably indebted to the Hobbits strange world in the Shire.

The roots

But Tolkein didn't just conjure up his adventures out of thin air. He readily admitted turning to the Icelandic sagas, ancient Celtic myths, the Nordic Viking sagas and other similar mythological tales as a solid source of inspiration.

Looking at the Icelandic Sagas, for instance, Njal's Saga, we encounter all the drama you could imagine. Here are noble knights, evil marauding princes, beautiful virgins and deceitful womenfolk. Here are lofty competitions and cunning assaults. Here a man is a man and a word is a word.

The 19th century witnessed a re-emergence of the folktale. In Norway we have Asbjørnsen & Moe, in Germany the fairy tales of the Brothers Grimm, in fact, everywhere in the Western world (and the eastern for that matter) people have each their own legends and their own more or less colourful fairy tales. Filled with dramatic events, sagacious wisdom and moral purpose.

Denmark has also had its folktales. They are a part of our cultural baggage. With or without trolls and princesses, with or without Vikings. The ancient myths of the gods, with Odin and Thor and their world in Midgård, have been the fairy tales for generations of Danish people. And obviously H.C. Andersen belongs right there in that rarefied element.

The fairy tales' illustration

Fairy tales have always been able to stand alone, yet nevertheless the finest illustrators in the country have often depicted them. For instance, in our corner of the world, Louis Moe, whose drawings for the Nordic myths of the gods and the great Viking sagas, is still to this day unsurpassed in his interpretations. Sensible and heroizing at the same time.

In recent times the distinguished Danish illustrators, Arne Ungermann and Ib Spang Olsen, have also interpreted the major fairy tales. Contrarily, there have been fewer painters that have dared try their interpretive hand at tackling the fairy tales.

One could ask: Have there actually been any painters who have wrestled with the imaginative form of the fairy tale? Yes and no.

We must name the symbolists, who in several ways verged on the fantastical style in their paintings. The literary critic Valdemar Vedel followed Danish symbolism very closely. He wrote characteristically: "The artists must pour their hearts out of what they have felt and thought and sought after, and courageously draw a world that their dreams have contrived, and their varying moods have coloured."

The symbolists

One of that times eminent symbolists was – in his own whimsical fashion – the painter J.F. Willumsen (1863-1958). Grandiose, he was rightly called. He was, in a variety of ways, a renaissance man and an incredibly many-faceted artist.

In 1892 he travelled to Norway, sailing along the coast all the way to the Lofoten Islands. With inspiration gathered from this trip he painted the large picture "Jotunheim", a fantastic and dramatic painting of the Jotunheim Mountains. But the painting wasn't just a mountainscape; it became a symbolic representation of nature's omnipotence. He later wrote about his impressions: "The clouds lifted and I found myself at the edge of a precipice looking out over a mountainous landscape of the high north, menacingly and brutally covered with eternal ice and snow, a world uninhabitable for people. Affected by this mood of gravity, the mind-pictures composed themselves in relief."

While some of the period's symbolists, such as the painters Viggo Pedersen and Johan Rohde, exhibited with a greater decorative beauty, there were others who were more directly connected with the fantastic. For instance Niels Skovgaard, who, among other things, was interested in the reigning romantic ideals found in folksongs.

But even more fabulous was the married couple Agnes and Harald Slott-Møller. They were totally absorbed in the beautiful and the romantic, even though Harald Slott-Møller could also paint social realistic pictures with a vengeance. But today we remember, for example, Agnes Slott-Møller's romantic painting of "Jomfru Blidelil" ("The Virgin Blidelil"), an angel who is flying over the beautiful sea.

Of the same generation we have the painter Poul S. Christiansen, whose paintings of, for instance, Dante at the gates of Hell, are sublimely fabulous. Johannes Holbæk, also an eccentric painter, mastered a fantastic and decorative style influenced by religiousness and spirituality. Joakim Skovgård is also important and must be named in this connection for his visionary religious paintings.

The new fantastics

Many people would probably say today that time has run out for the fantastic painting. The last remnants washed away by modernism. The romantic painting, as known from the Victorian era in England, is today only a curious footnote in art history even though many collectors are interested in the period and the genre.

The essentially different and classical surrealism has always been there, right up until today. Magical realism was, as stated earlier quickly fenced off and banished to a corner of art history. In recent years there has been a lot of talk instead about fantastic figuration, which is basically just an imprecise umbrella term for realistic painters who maintain a figurative expression, mixing it up with more fantastic elements.

But there are always painters appearing on the scene who swim against the current. As an example, Martin Bigum in

Denmark. Perceived by many as a cartoonish and humorous painter, he is really an artist who takes the fantastic seriously. But also painters like Chr. Schmidt-Rasmussen and Katrine Ærtebjerg have more than flirted with a fantastic universe, although in completely different ways.

Frello the misfit

Otto Frello (b. 1924) is one of the genuine Danish fantastic painters. He studied art history at the University of Copenhagen for a couple of years and took drawing and painting classes at the large, private art school "Akadamiet for fri og merkantil kunst" (The Academy for Free and Commercial Art). He stayed in Paris for a short time where he drew sculptures at the Louvre. After returning to Denmark he started teaching at the aforementioned art school, where for the next sixteen years he taught thousands of students to draw and paint.

While still teaching, Otto Frello made a living as an illustrator. He worked for, among others, The Armed Forces ABC School and Kellogg's Cornflakes. Also Politiken's publishing house employed him for a series of handbooks such as "Birds in Colour", "Precious Stones in Colour" etc. He was a very precise and meticulous illustrator who loved filling in all the details in his drawings.

This work awoke in him a pressing desire to paint and he threw himself into a long series of freely fabulating paintings. Almost just for fun he sent some of these paintings to Kunsternes Efterårsudstilling (The Artists Autumn Exhibition), where to his utter amazement they were accepted. But otherwise Frello kept himself far away from the art world (and the art world kept itself far away from him). Right from the start he was declared a misfit. Out of step with his time.

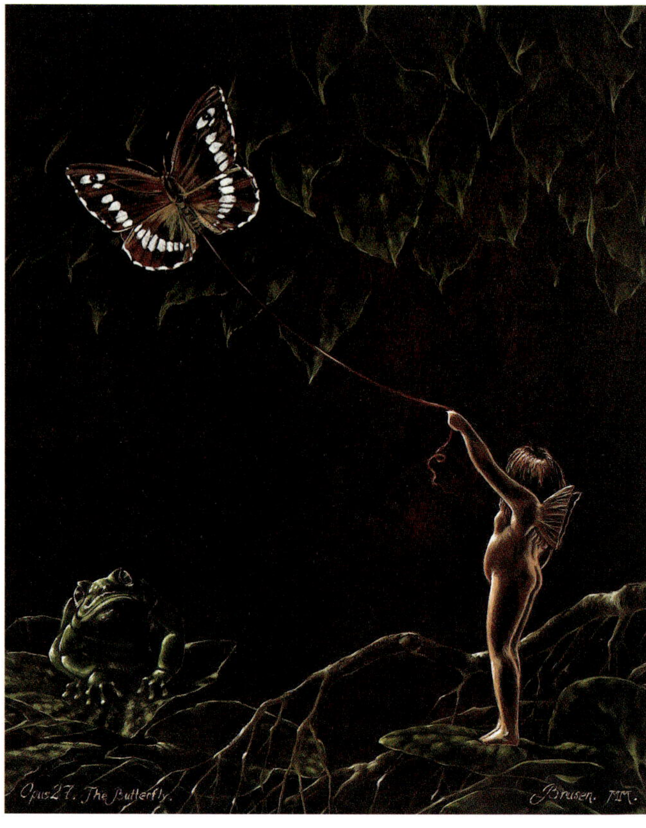

Opus 27
Butterfly
Oil on Panel
size 20 x 16 cm
2000

Fantastic realism

But his obscurity didn't last, and in December 1989 he was able to open a large exhibition at the Varde Museum (an exhibition that created a sensation across the country. And again in 2004) in honour of his 80th birthday, there was another large exhibition of his work in Varde and Copenhagen, respectively.

Otto Frello has always astonished us. In 1997 he agreed to paint a large picture, a panorama of the primeval forest that existed 40 million years ago and is the source of all the amber we find along our coasts. He has also built a two-meter high model of a Jugend house complete with fantastic details.

The critics have always had a hard time trying to pigeonhole Frello. Is his work surrealism, magical realism or fantastic realism? Not really any of them. He does acknowledge a debt to claire-obscure and trompe l'oeil centuries old styles/techniques.

A painter like Claus Brusen undoubtedly owes a great deal to Otto Frello. But there is another Danish painter who has been just as significant, namely Carsten Svennson. He was originally trained as a typographer but began painting in his spare time. His style is surrealistic and yet satirical of society at the same time. With more than ancestral roots stretching back to Hieronymus Bosch, Pieter Breughel and Albrecht Dürer.

The foreigners

But we must look abroad to find a number of artists who had a great significance for Brusen.

First and foremost is the English painter Patrick Woodroofe, who is considered to be one of the most widely acclaimed artists of the fantastic genre. He was born in Cornwall, studied literature at Leeds University and then began to teach. He spent his spare time painting and drawing and gradually it got the upper hand. He was involved in making the background scenery for Michael Ende's famous fantasy "The Neverending Story", but it is as a painter that he's become world famous. Woodroofe's imaginative paintings are full of flying cows, upside down mountains, petite peculiar princesses, monsters, ancient castles and strange landscapes.

There are many others, for instance, the Russian Sergei Aparin, whose pictures are based on crazy Russian folktales. Or the American painter David Bowers, whose paintings are an odd mixture of old Renaissance painting and modern science fiction illustrations. Bowers was educated at the Art Institute of Pittsburgh and has exhibited throughout the world.

Other names to be named are Steven Kenny, Boris Vallejo, Bruno de Maio and Gil Brunel. All fantastic painters – and illustrators. And all of them difficult to place because they have let their wildest fantasies run rampant. A bit overdone, will the more cautious think. But exaggeration does indeed enhance understanding.

The art of illustration

It is characteristic that painters of fantastical art have often been classified as just illustrators (real meaning: not genuine artists). Simply because they don't fit into any of the artistic genres we normally deal with.

Also here there are names that stand out. The American Joe Frazetta and the French Philippe Druillet are examples of contemporary cartoonists whose illustrative artwork is of the highest order, yet they must still resign themselves to being ignored by the "real" art world.

A painter like Claus Brusen undoubtedly owes a great deal to the best elements of the art of illustration.

When all's said and done it might be just his luck to find himself in a setting where there are no rules and where all the arbiters of taste have long gone home, bewilderedly shaking their heads because their usual solutions don't work here.

Chapter 2

Sometime in the Fantasy

It all started with a wish to do anything else than have an ordinary job!

This is how Claus Brusen himself explains how he later became an artist. He originally wanted to be a musician, but as he suffered from stage fright it didn't work out. Subsequently he threw himself into art.

Claus Brusen, throughout his childhood, laid the foundation by spending all his time drawing. While the others wrote essays or did something else in school, he drew. When he got home from school, he drew then too. Small figures and strange creatures.

When he was sixteen, things really got going. This was the time when everyone covered their walls with posters, and there is one artist whom he especially remembers for some profoundly fascinating pictures, namely Salvador Dali, the great Spanish surrealist.

Coloured drawings

Claus Brusen now became serious about his drawing and for the first time he tried his hand at a little more complicated compositions. It turned into a long series of surrealistic drawings that he coloured in afterwards.

In 1978 he attempted his first oil painting. He had seen others do it so why not try himself. By the way, he still has that first painting hanging in his living room. It was a classical surrealistic motif where all the elements were floating around between each other.

But why did he turn to surrealism?

"There was something impertinent and provocative in the imagery and the way of creating a whole new world. I have always really liked paintings that resembled something, but when you paint surrealistically, you break all the limits. And that attracted me, although I really couldn't explain why. But it's the fascination of being able to create your own entire universe, where, like some kind of God, you could decide which peculiar things happened, that has surely always been deep inside me.

Record covers

Another source of inspiration for Claus Brusen came from record covers. He saw covers by artists such as Roger Dean and others whose brilliant strokes he was crazy about.

Salvador Dali appeared again. His posters were hanging everywhere and Claus Brusen visited the library and found books about the artist. Here he came across other surrealists who painted in the same style and a whole new world opened up for him. And on the same occasion he started considering becoming an artist. He even thought about applying to The Art Academy (Kunstakademiet), but a little birdie told him that if he began painting surrealistically there, he would be thrown out. So he stopped thinking about it.

Censored exhibitions

Instead, he began sending pictures to a succession of different censored exhibits: The Free (Den Frie), Charlottenborg, etc. Time after time they came right back to him and now he began seriously considering not continuing like this. Besides, it was expensive each time he had to send the pictures off. Now that the system was so rejective, he started thinking about entirely different possibilities. For a short time he had a romantic dream of buying a cottage somewhere on Funen (Fyn), let his wife go to work, and then he could stay home and paint. They wound up buying the cottage but were there for just a few months before they nevertheless decided to return to Sæby in Northern Jutland.

Once back he got an unremarkably respectable job as a clerk in a drug store. And he resigned himself to having to work during the day and devoted himself to his altogether special hobby in the evening. "It suited me just fine," recalls Claus Brusen.

The struggle to create

But surrealism was giving him a real hard time. "It was a struggle each time to come up with something new that was even more fantastic than the last one. I spent oodles of time trying to think up new and different things. Preferably there should be a brand new composition every time I sat down in front of the canvas. I was using way too much energy and I always had the feeling that maybe it just wasn't quite enough."

But Claus Brusen had always been engrossed by the world of fairy tales, and yet, in spite of that, he thought that just maybe it was a bit too kitschy. He had earlier been aware of Patrick Woodroffe and other great illustrators. Their imagery touched him in a very special way. Their delight in drawing, their artistic ability – something, that for Claus Brusen conflicted with surrealism, which he more and more perceived as "negative" and "scoffing". More like bad nightmares than good dreams.

Cartoons never became a major source of inspiration for him, although he still considers Carl Banks from Walt Disney a great master. "I have always regarded cartoons as a separate art form, and I just can't do it."

The fantastic

It was now obvious for Claus Brusen that he had to get away from surrealism and into a more fantastically good-natured universe. He was finally on the right track.

"I suddenly felt like a God in my own universe. I made the rules myself about how this world should work…," recalls Claus Brusen, and continues: "It also gives responsibilities, because you have to make sure that it is a just world. I've slowly come to the opinion that the crueler the real world becomes, the nicer my pictures become. My pictures will be a contrast to all the cruelty we meet in our daily lives."

But he does admit that there are ambiguities in his pictures. It can't be avoided, for once in a while it's like the small beings one meets in his universe have a say in the matter.

The erotic – and the naïve

The erotic also plays a certain role in his universe, as he well admits. "Ah, but it's almost a genetic character trait that men love to look at the woman's naked body. That's all it is, and yes, it is erotic. But it's really just a question of the female body having some beautiful forms that are quite unique," I feel. As seen through his eyes, with human beings it's the woman who is beautiful, while with the animals it is most often the male who is the prettiest.

"Call it erotic, if you will, but let me say that it is perfectly natural for my small male figures to look at naked women!"

Claus Brusen regards his Lilliputian world as a "totally naïve world". A colleague once teasingly remarked that his picture world was a place where you got the feeling that the menu consisted solely of strawberries and strawberries and strawberries. "I didn't feel offended by it, for nature and the love of nature is central to me," says the artist.

A Paradise

Claus Brusen views his world as a paradise. A closed world where the forces of good rule.

He believes we all have a dream of paradise inside us. A dream that has lain dormant since childhood. A dream where beauty, balance, harmony and joy are essential ingredients.

"I also see the nude as a symbol of the beautiful. Not beautiful in a sexual sense, but beautiful in the sense that it is original and genuine. The nude is a special form of poetry. And in a fairy tale world like mine everything is beautiful, even an old tree, just like an old person can be beautiful."

Symbols

Surrealism was known for its close connection with psychoanalysis and its interpretation of symbols. But as we know, symbols go even further back in history. From the oldest cultures on earth we see the use of symbols, which is also reflected in the many legends and fairy tales.

Claus Brusen also uses symbols in his fantastic pictures. They're in his choice of colour, in the composition and in the selection of certain figures and objects, and their mutual relations. But he won't provide you with the answers. Part of the fascination with his work is you can go exploring also for symbols.

But the artist emphasizes that even though there are many symbols in his pictures, they are not there for the symbols' sake. It's just as much Brusen wanting to "tease" his viewers by placing elements in the pictures that can't be quickly decoded.

The forest as a universe

But where do Claus Brusen's ideas come from?

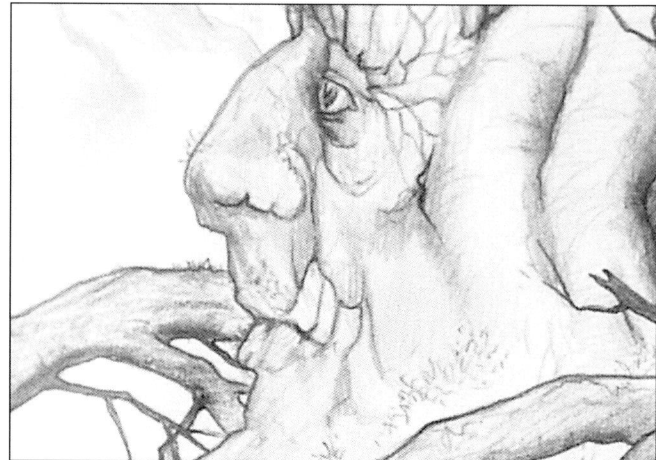

Drawing (detail)

"From the pictures themselves. Earlier pictures give birth to ideas for new pictures. From my imagination. Today I can't hold the pictures back at all, they just burst forth as opposed to my surrealistic period, where I had to struggle to call forth the pictures. Many of my pictures start on the forest floor. Here is an entire world. Look down and imagine what can take place on a thick forest floor! Or look up and imagine what can take place in the dense foliage of the trees….. or in the depths of the forest, along its edge. A forest, you see, is a universe, just so abundant," says Claus Brusen.

The pictures are created

The story nearly always pops up by itself. Maybe it starts with a figure that is portrayed. An atmosphere that is implied. And that's that. It's often in the small pictures, which are often precursors of the larger ones. Therefore, we can say that taken together, Claus Brusen's many pictures comprise a large and intricate tale.

The large paintings always tell a story. It is often complicated and can have several interweaving scenarios.

A moral universe

The artist makes no secret of the fact that his universe is a highly moral one. That there are certain ground rules is obvious. No matter how odd or ugly or different they are, the figures and characters are respectful of each other. There is also a great respect for nature in his pictures.

"But I don't want to moralize or be a know-it-all, and I don't think an artist should. But you may certainly regard my universe as a beautiful, romantic dream, a kind of fantastic utopia," says Claus Brusen.

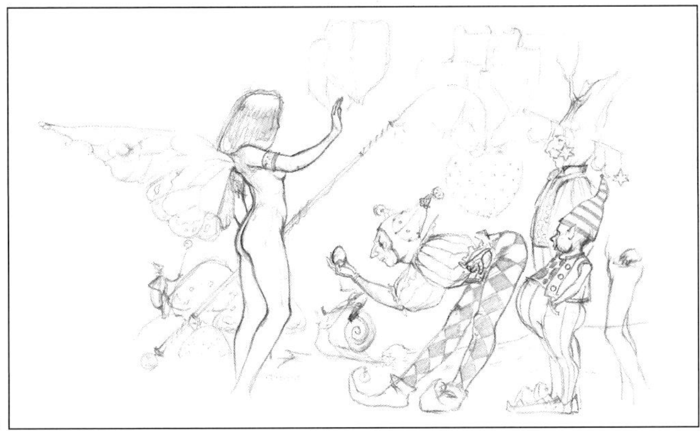

Sketch

Chapter 3

The Fantastical

Vladimir Soloviov, the Russian philosopher and mystic, attempted to describe and limit the concept of "the fantastic" in several of his works. He wrote, among other things, "An outer and formal possibility for a simple explanation of the phenomena is always maintained in the real fantastic, but at the same time this explanation is divested of all inner probability."

The English author (and ghost expert) Montague Rhodes James, always the provoker: "It is sometimes necessary to leave the door open for a natural explanation, but let me add: this opening might be so narrow you can't get through it."

The French author Castex also attempted a definition: "The fantastic is characterized by the mystery's brutal intrusion into the realm of real life." Meaning: There is a contradiction between the fantastic and the real. And furthermore: The fantastic threatens sensible reality.

A genre?

If the fantastic is a genre can de debated. In any case it's a broad definition, whether we are talking about literature, film or the pictorial arts.

The obscure and the sinister have existed within literature for centuries in the form of horror stories, ghost stories and so-called tales about other strange beings. A lot of these tales have become part of the oral storytelling traditon, told in the dark to gatherings around a fire or an oil lamp. When the tree branches scratched at the windows, there wasn't any doubt that something was afoot that the light of day couldn't reveal. The listeners could shudder with good reason, for there was more between heaven and earth than reason dictated.

In our time vampire and werewolf movies have had a large following, just as horror movies about giant apes, monster spiders and other creatures, possibly from outer space, have scared us out of our wits.

H.G. Wells and other suspense writers of that time fabulated about attacks from outer space while Conan Doyle wrote about a hidden island where prehistoric monsters still roamed – and, all in all, that era was full of those types of stories. Often these tales had the sole intention of chocking and scaring the readers, as when the great master of horror, Edgar Allan Poe, described the more diabolical and supernatural sides of life.

Religion's downside

The Church and religion also had its share of the honor for the dark superstition. The witch-burning fires blazed throughout Europe during the Middle Ages. The priests spoke warningly of devils and demons as something that threatened every good Christian, and was especially a danger to those of little faith. The courts of the Inquisition were established and people were encouraged to report witches to the authorities.

Christianity forged ahead and popular superstition was denounced. But this didn't eradicate the belief in the supernatural. The only thing the Church got out of its persistent propaganda was probably just a few more people believing in things like that.

The dream about the fantastic

In 1298 the adventurer Marco Polo published his memoirs wherein he tells of his incredible travels and all the curiosities he encountered. He tells us, among other things, about the Malabar coast where he came across the kingdom of Coilo. Here the explorer meets a population that has some peculiar habits – like collecting strange peppers that they use for both food and medicine. But in addition the country houses some weird creatures, for example Blemmas creatures without heads and with mouths in the middle of their stomachs. Another type of creature was the Sciapode, an animal-like being that lay resting in the shadow of its own foot. And finally there were the Monocles creatures with one enormous eye that could see everything, even at great distances.

Some years later, in 1372, the author John Mandeville published his "Treatise on the most wonderful and remarkable things that exist in the world". Perhaps a dubious book that just like Polo's tells of peculiar, unknown species of animals from around the world. The author himself hadn't actually seen these remarkable creatures he described, but it was certain that they existed.

Gnomes and other small folk

The gnome was a classic figure in popular superstition. The little people, as the gnomes were also called, were especially active in the counryside. They were shy and seldom seen by people. They could have enormous strength and by the way, very close to animals. One should preferably leave porridge for them on Christmas eve, and sure enough, the porridge would be gone the next morning..

Of course there were also trolls – of different varieties. Large beasts that could get it into their heads to throw boulders at church steeples – and small, more jovial forest trolls that could lickety-split disappear under a bush. Trolls could be hot-tempered and evil, but there were also good-natured and friendly types that would let themselves be seen by people every now and then.

There were elves that danced throughout the night on their mounds, where they also practiced their magic. All sensible people should beware of the elves. They were beautiful, but hollow when seen from the back (which exposed them), and tried in the most cunning ways to entice people. If you fell for them you could risk insanity, or groggily return home several years after what you thought had been just one night of reckless dancing.

The evil powers

There were many other evil powers at work. There were witches flying through the air on their brooms or out in the night time meadows concocting their witches' brew of frogs, snakes and other disgusting ingredients with which to poison sensible people. You could fly if you rubbed witches' salve on your back. And witches could turn into black ravens and vicious dogs that could move around at night with unnatural speed.

According to all popular superstitions, the evil powers exist everywhere. There are places where you shouldn't go, and never at night. Especially graveyards and former gallows hills are dangerous places.

Occultism or superstition

In the world of the occult there were much worse and more terrifying creatures, such as ghosts and apparitions and that sort of supernatural beings. Demons and devils ready to pounce, and you have to be very careful about not attracting their attention, if so, you are lost.

In his book "The Insight's place" (Indsigtens sted), the writer Erwin Neutsky-Wulff describes how satanists can invoke evil spirits with certain ritual actions that typically unfold within a large pentagram. The Old Testament and Christian view that blood was the seat of the soul is also believed by satanists. That is why they drink blood at satanic masses. Of animals like roosters or goats – or even worse, of newly butchered babies.

Fabulous and fantastic painting has, throughout history, relied heavily on precisely this occult knowledge that, among other sources, originated from secret occult brotherhoods like e.g. The Golden Dawn and The Order of the Knights Templar.

The occult symbolism used for centuries by these occult brotherhoods is also found in abundance in the fanatastic painting. A symbolism we also see utilized in the field of heraldry.

Many painters of the fantastic have also gained inspiration from the ancient cards of prophecy, the Tarot-cards, which are a condensed version of a thousand year old occult wisdom.

Inspiration and contrast

The occult is a rich source of inspiration for the fantastic painters. Regardless of how heretical or exaggerated many of the occult theories appear, they often simply contain all the sensational ingredients that so many find exciting, mysterious and enticing.

The new renaissance that fantastic art has experienced is certainly connected with the grey boredom of everday life. Political life is more and more just talking suits. The large international companies, controllers of politics and our consumption, are just as dull as their one-track venture for maximizing profits.

In this scenario the fairy tale plays an important role as both protest and escape from reality. Here is a world that is poetic, mysterious and enticing.

Chapter 4

Dream and Nightmare

An incubus is a frightening demon that comes at night and sits on sleeping peoples' chests and causes them to have the most horrifying dreams. A motif that many painters have thrown themselves into. Here in Denmark we know, among others, N.A. Abildgaard's famous picture of a small demon sitting on a sleeping woman's chest.

All in all, the night is the place where the imagination can take unexpected and often terrifying turns. The English author, Bruce Chatwin, has argued that there is a concrete, historical reason for darkness, nighttime and evil being inextricably connected in human consciousness.

At night most people feel extra exposed. They are afraid of loneliness and the cold and they're afraid of being attacked. This is historical knowledge, inherited through centuries. A kind of collective knowledge, hidden away in each and every person.

It is this terror that hibernates in the child's instinctive fear of the dark and of the powers that the darkness hides.

Evil sees you

As we grow older we learn to control this fear. Yet it is always lurking on the fringe of our consciousness and lots of adults must admit that they suffer from a certain fear of darkness. Whether it is deeply irrational or not.

Fear can be diffuse, and that's why we often dress it in certain figures (e.g. borrowed from childhood's fairy tales). The American psychoanalyst A.A.Mason has described this particular and universal form of fear that arises in the dark:

"It creates a feeling of being watched by eyes that nothing escapes from. These eyes are gruesome, penetrating, inhuman and intent. They watch you mercilessly, without pity or compassion. They follow you everywhere and judge you unscrupulously. You cannot escape from them, for there is nowhere to run to. They remember everything and their threat is all-embracing. The punishment will hit you like a flash, destructive and merciless....".

You can call this a form of primeval fear that can assume many forms and many shapes. And it is a fear that is often flirted with in the fantastic painting.

The anatomy of the dream

We dream, therefore we are. If we didn't dream we would go insane. In the special world of dreams, anything can happen. Logic doesn't rule here and time, space and people are contorted to the unrecognizable.

In dreams we can find ourselves in several times at the same time. We mix people we know all together: Fathers, lovers, mothers and sweethearts. We fly, or move wildly about without being able to get anywhere.

Dreams are, the truth be told, surrealistic.

Throughout his life, the English ghost researcher, M.R. James, (he was provost at the famous English boarding school Eton) collected accounts from people who had experienced extraordinary things. A man, believing himself bewitched by his enemy,

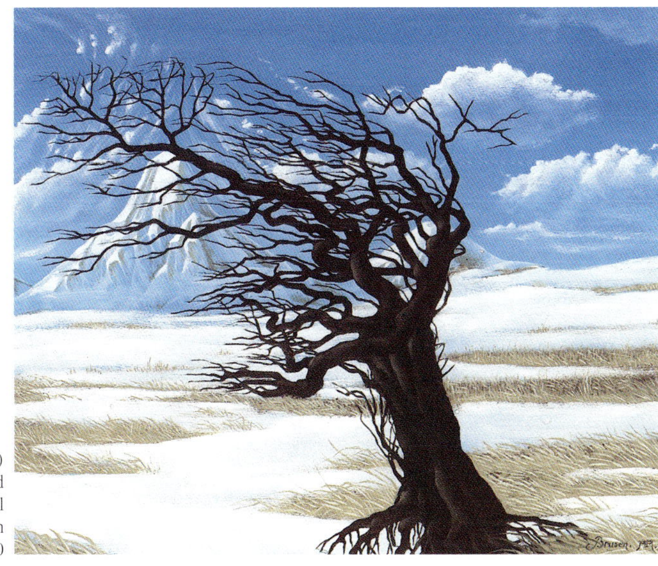

Opus 17 (detail)
The Northern Wasteland
Oil on Panel
size 20 x 30 cm
2000

reached in under his pillow to get his watch but instead got hold of according to the man's own information, "a mouth with teeth, and with hair around it….. not a mouth from a human". An anxious little boy, who was treated for his serious anxiety attacks, told of a recurring nightmare: The pillow he slept with at night turned out to have a big mouth that suddenly opened up and ate his head.

The English psychiatrist John Cheever published the diary entries of a patient who suffered extensively from nightmares. The patient describes his dreams (nightmares) like this: "We see three worlds – the night, the day and the night in the night. Here we find the deads' passions and ambitions, maliciously and powerfully wandering about among us. A world of open graves. A world in which our conceptual ability comes up short. We possess no names, no forms, no light, no color to fill out these forces, and yet they are as powerful as the living."

The dream's vision

Of course dreams are also good dreams and entertaining dreams. Dreams are flights of the imagination, a ticket to other worlds. The surrealist painter Leonora Carrington once said: "I've always had access to other worlds. We all do, because we all dream. It's myself I don't have access to."

Dreams, and their lack of reason and logic, often catch the interest of psychologists and psychiatrists. It is here we meet hallucinations, odd notions and delusions. The philosopher Schopenhauer thought that "the dream is a short-lasting madness, madness a long dream".

But dreams are also driven by passion. They are pleasureful, just as daydreams can be. They consist of burning desires and magnificent visions of a better world. A world that is precisely so innocent and natural as the one we observe in the painter Claus Brusen's pictures. With small, friendly beings living in harmony with nature and in harmony with their own curiosity. In touch with their desires (the naked elves) and the beautiful surroundings where the forest, in a manner of speaking, embraces its inhabitants.

The dream of Nactalius is clearly such a desirous dream. A dream we yearn to allow ourselves to slip into.

Chapter 5

Fantasy and Vision

The dream of a better world is oftentimes the motivating force in fairy tales. Here there is a difference between good and evil. Here good wins over evil. You are really never in doubt about whom is whom. You can see it. Here there are noble emotions at risk and life is a series of dramas that everybody can understand and relate to because they are clear-cut. Meanness is punished and bravery rewarded.

Utopia is the dream of the beautiful and humane future society where all is idyllic and people live in eternal peace with each other.

The future has its beautiful visions and its shadowy nightmares. We meet these two contrasting elements time and time again in classic science fiction literature.

Ray Bradbury, the great classic science fiction author, tells us, in his first large collection of short stories "The Martian Chronicles", how a spaceship from outer space lands on a beach. The well-armed crew is ready to disembark and destroy everything they see when a big family dog suddenly slurps them up in one mouthful! (the dangerous spaceship wasn't all that big).

The unexpected can topple even the most perilous invasion.

The good vision

But science fiction literature also includes more paradise-like descriptions where people or uncommon beings live in a peaceful idyll, without greed or cruel capitalism to ruin everything.

There is also talk about speculative literature that fabricates unique universes where people and state-of-the-art technology work together in perfect harmony. The myth of Atlantis, the most well known of these figments of the imagination, depicts a mythical realm where good, truth and beauty have triumphed.

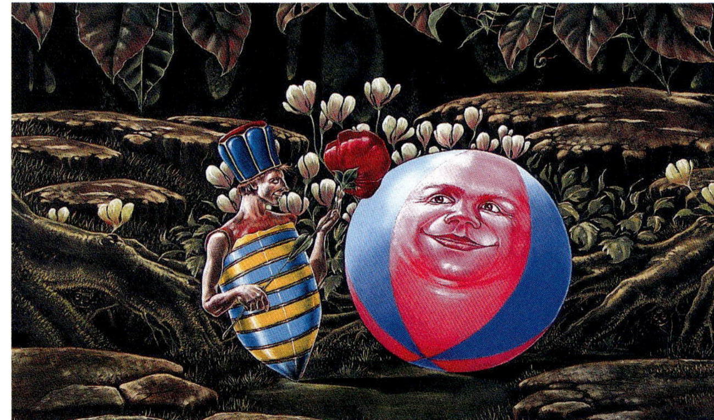

Lovers (detail)
Oil on Panel
size 28 x 36 cm
2005
Inspired by the story of H.C. A

Chapter 6

Dreams never-ending

Nactalius is the place that isn't. A fictive land where people are not allowed. It's like Peter Pan's well-known island Neverland, somewhere out there in space. Anything can happen here, as in a dream.

Or is it there anyway, somewhere out there, on the edge of our consciousness. Like a hidden thought. Outside of reason's dispassionate reach? We never really get an answer. And actually, Brusen is not at all such a moralist as to pontificate to us.

But his universe is in many ways a lustful and playful universe. As for instance seen in the picture "Opus 10. A gentle touch of conversation", where we again find ourselves out in the green, lush forest where naked elves flirtingly gambol about and the small toadstool-clad dwarfish beings are busy. One of them stands there with a mischievous look and pokes a naked and rather voluptuous elven girl's derrière.

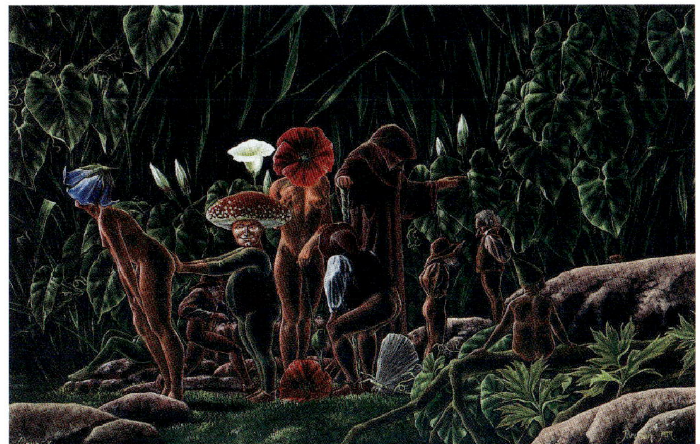

Opus 10
...tle touch of Conversation
Oil on Panel
size 20 x 30 cm
2000

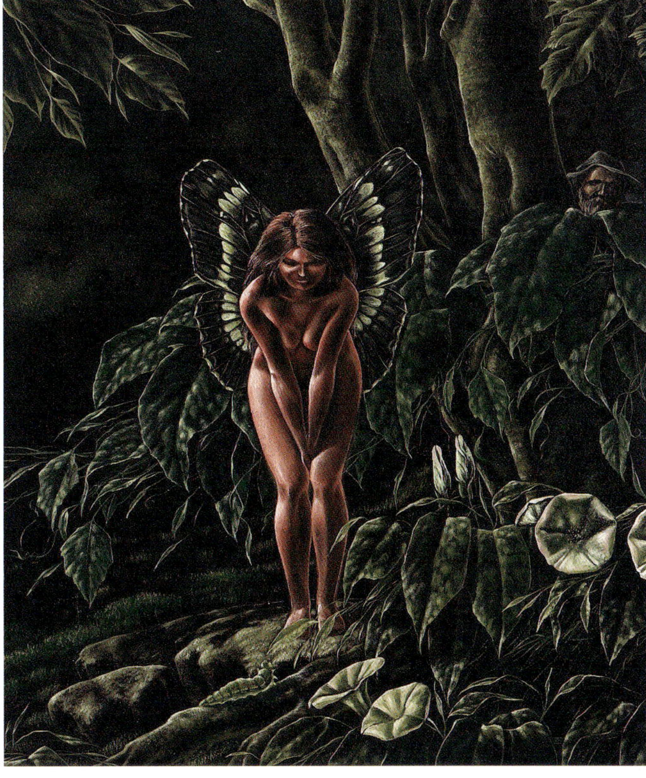

Opus 31
Nephelia
Oil on Panel
size 30 x 20 cm
2001

Innocence prevails, and yet not at all. For if you look closely there is quite a bit that points in an absolutely non-innocent direction: There is a dwarfish person standing with his back to us regarding another naked elven girl who is coquettishly covering her loins with one hand while covering her face with a big flower. And a little, naked male figure is sitting on a green branch gazing mirthfully into the forest. Another small manikin is frenetically running on his way – to where is uncertain.

The whole scene contains eroticism and humour. And a lot more questions than answers.

The enigmatic

It is characteristic of Claus Brusen's universe to contain one puzzle after another. It's as if it is his intention to tease the observer and keep him or her in the dark. All his small beings in the land of Nactalius aren't easy to figure out.

They are friendly, indeed, but certainly not without their more ambiguous aspects. Like unruly teasing spirits that can't or won't be controlled.

In Claus Brusen's depictions it is often just one quite simple subtlety he employs. As when a beautiful, naked elven girl with butterfly wings is looking delightedly at a little green caterpillar. But the picture changes character when we see a man's face lurking in the bushes behind her.

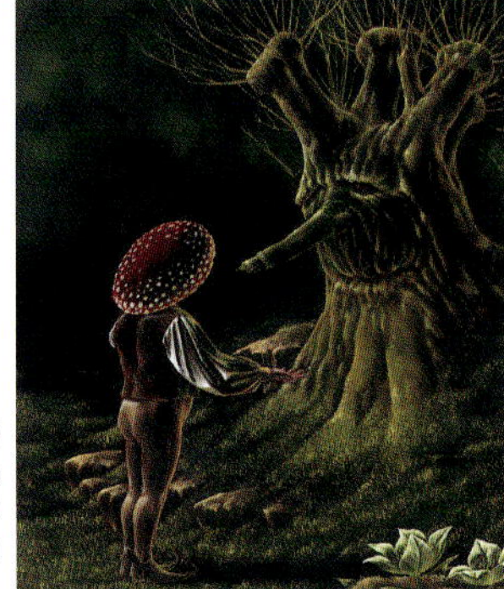

Opus 36
Old and Wise
Oil on Panel
size 30 x 20 cm
2001

The picture "Old and Wise" is simpler, just a little toadstool-hat wearing manikin standing and listening to words of wisdom from an old gnarled tree. And again it is one of the pictures that sets the observer's imagination in motion. What is being talked about? What is the tree telling the little toadstool-hat man?

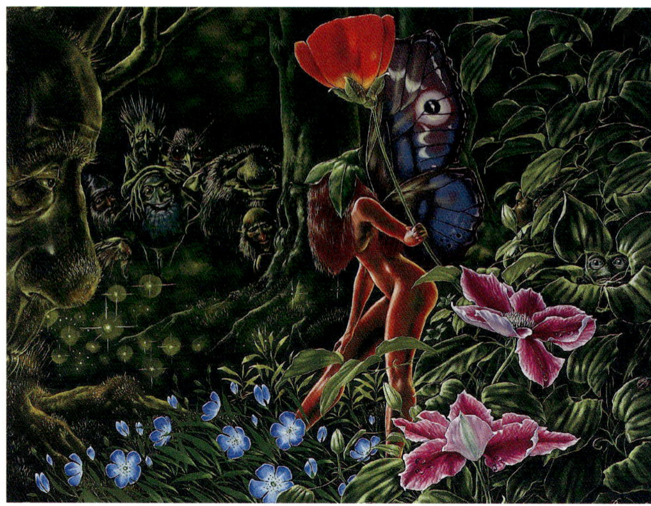

Opus 100
Audience
Oil on Panel
size 40 x 50 cm
2003

The spirit of nature

Claus Brusen's fantastic picture world encompasses another ancient element known from numerous fairy tales and old legends, and that is the myth of "the spirit of nature" (pantheism). It is an old and persistent myth that stems from the first primitive people that inhabited the earth. They believed in nature as a living entity. The divine was, in a manner of speaking, built into nature's smallest creatures and objects.

Plants were living beings. If you cut a branch off a tree it was like mutilating a sentient being. If you plucked a flower, you murdered it. If there were thunderstorms, then nature was showing its anger, etc. Therefore, special rituals were demanded to get along in the natural world.

This primitive belief has wandered over into most of the old fairy tales, and in fact also into Claus Brusen's picture world. We see it, for example, in his painting "Opus 100: Audiens" ("Opus 100: Audience") from 2003, where a naked elven girl is standing in the middle of the forest. She's holding a beautiful, red flower in one hand. In the left side of the picture lurks a large, green tree-man and peering in the background is a row of even stranger beings: a troll, yet another forest creature, a gnome, an owl-like bird, et al. It looks like they have grown right up of the forest floor. They are both threatening and friendly at the same time.

In an earlier picture from 2002, "Opus 90: Nature gives, and we are grateful", the metaphor of nature is even more obvious. Here is a large group of the forest's peculiar beings gathered around a pile of fruit: cherries, strawberries, apples and more, as in a celebration. The mood among these denizens of the forest is cheerful, almost wanton. Are we talking about a fertility cult, or what?

In Claus Brusen's universe nakedness is just as natural as is meeting familiar and unfamiliar animals and other creatures side by side. It's as though, just like explorers, we are visiting a remote and incomprehensible culture deep in the forest far removed from civilisation. A culture that has its own to us indecipherable rules.

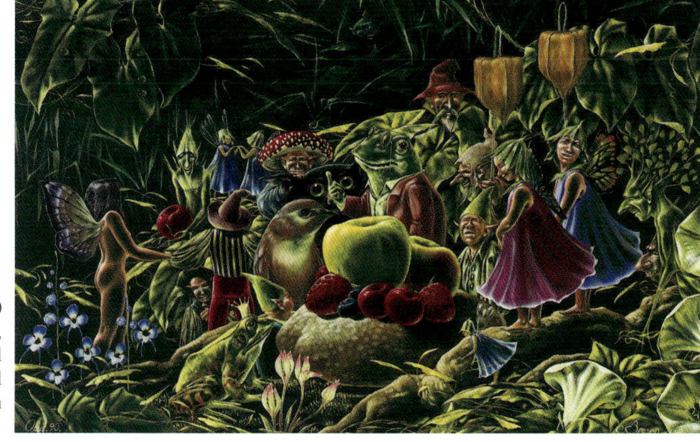

Opus 90
Nature gives,
and we are Greatful
Oil on Panel
size 30 x 20 cm
2001

Chapter 7

Happily ever after

Once upon a time. And it's far from over yet. It's only just begun. The adventure of fantastical painting and its proliferation.

Denmark is a very small part of a big world. Denmark is the country where H.C. Andersen wrote his fairy tales that later became known throughout the world. Otherwise there is not so much else that we are known for.

We have perhaps only a handful of painters that have thrown themselves into the wondrous and fantastic painting. Maybe they are pioneers in a type of painting that we will see a lot more of in the future.

They all have roots in surrealism, although they have distanced themselves from the first wave of surrealists in Denmark where Wilhelm Freddie and others set the agenda.

When magic realism (Danish version) popped up in Denmark in the late 1960's around Gallery Passepartout, among others, in central Copenhagen, there was an opening up toward the painting that we today call for lack of a better name, "the fantastical painting". The imagination to power was one of the slogans this group of artists used at the same time as they refined their painting toward the decorative and even more fabulating. But suddenly there was so much else going on in the world of art that magic realism, in reality, was "blacklisted". Some of the genre's practitioners later turned up under the collective name "fantastic figuration".

But the genre wasn't completely extinct. A painter like Otto Frello held on. Carsten Svennson perfected his special variation of surrealistic expression. In a corner of the country Stig Weye continued to paint his naively subtle and fabulating pictures. Jens Jalling appeared and turned everything in a more satirical direction. There were a few others, but still only a small group.

Until Claus Brusen appeared out of nowhere and presented his distinctive universe called Nactalius.

Where does it all end? We have yet to see the blossoming of this adventure.

This is for certain.

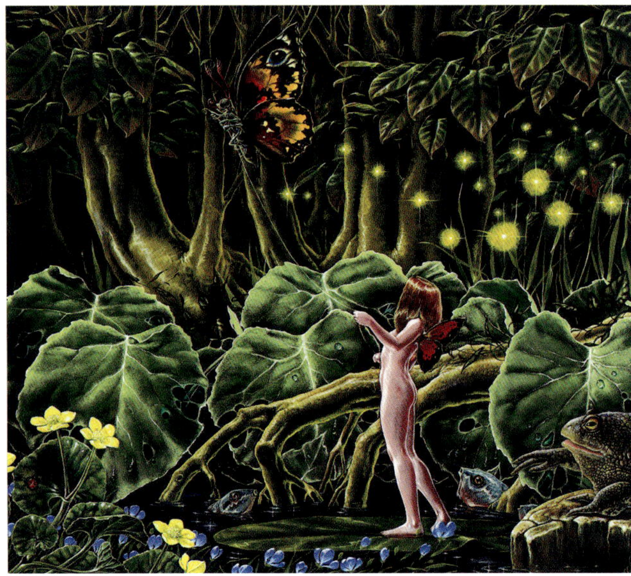

Thumbelina (detail)
Oil on Panel
size 40 x 50 cm
2005
Inspired by the story of H.C. Andersen

Artists Statemet

CLAUS BRUSEN. 1960 DENMARK
Autodidakt Painter

Once Upon a Time. That is how all fairytales start.

I started back in 1976, with drawings inspired by Salvador Dali, and of course by the Album covers in the seventies, especially artists like Patrick Woodroffe. Later I discovered the fantastic work by Michael Parkes which has that romantic dreamlike thing that I love so much. Claude Verlinde for his expression in the faces of his figures, and very dreamlike landscapes.

All three I admire for there fantastic skills, and wonderful sense for composition. Other inspiration sources are the Victorian painters, such as John Anser Fitzgerald and Richard Dadd. For many years I worked with the surreal expression "Dali/Ernst/Magritte." But always with the fascination for the world of Fairies and other little creatures. It was not until 1998 that the world of Nactalius. "The name of my own World." Started seriously and became the only thing I from then on worked with, I got the name Nactalius in a dream back in 1981, where I also made my first Fairy world painting, then the world was born.There where to be many years before I had the courage to paint like that again, but when I finally started, I knew it was the right thing for me to do, it seems like it never stops, the ideas are coming like I was never to stop again.

There are is great pleasure in painting this world, because it has a lot of parallels to our own world, which I enjoy describing, but I have chosen that there is no evil in my world. After all this is one of the advantages of creating an entire world of your own. We see to much evil as it is in our lifetime, so my little protest against that are, the more evil the world becomes, the sweeter my paintings become. This is my way of trying to keep a balance. The fascination of painting/creating is, you are able to create a world that is entirely your own, it is indeed the "Land of make-believe."

Claus Brusen
November 2005

Exhibitions:

1983 Art-Museum of Frederikshavn, Denmark
2001-03 Gallery Northwind, Denmark
2001 Gent Art Fair, Belgium
2002 Strassburg Art Fair, France
2002 Gallerigården, Denmark
2002 Stockholm Art fair, Sweden
2002-03 Copenhagen Art Fair, Denmark
2003 Gallery Max. Ystad, Sweden
2004-05 Galerie Michelle Boulet, Paris, France
2004 Interart Gallery, Manhattan NY, USA
2004 Chalk Farm Gallery, Santa Fe NM, USA
2004 Middle St. Gallery, Virginia Washington, USA
2005 Skive Art-Museum, Denmark
2005 H. C. Andersen+, Voergaard Castle, Denmark
2005 Cello festival, Kronberg im Taunus, Germany
2005 Skive Art-Museum, Denmark, Soloudstilling
2006 Galcric Honingcn, Gouda, The Netherlands

"I believe that the fairy tale has its own method of reflecting the truth."
J.R.R. Tolkien

OPUS 2

The Healing Tree

Oil on Wood • 20 x 30 cm • 2000

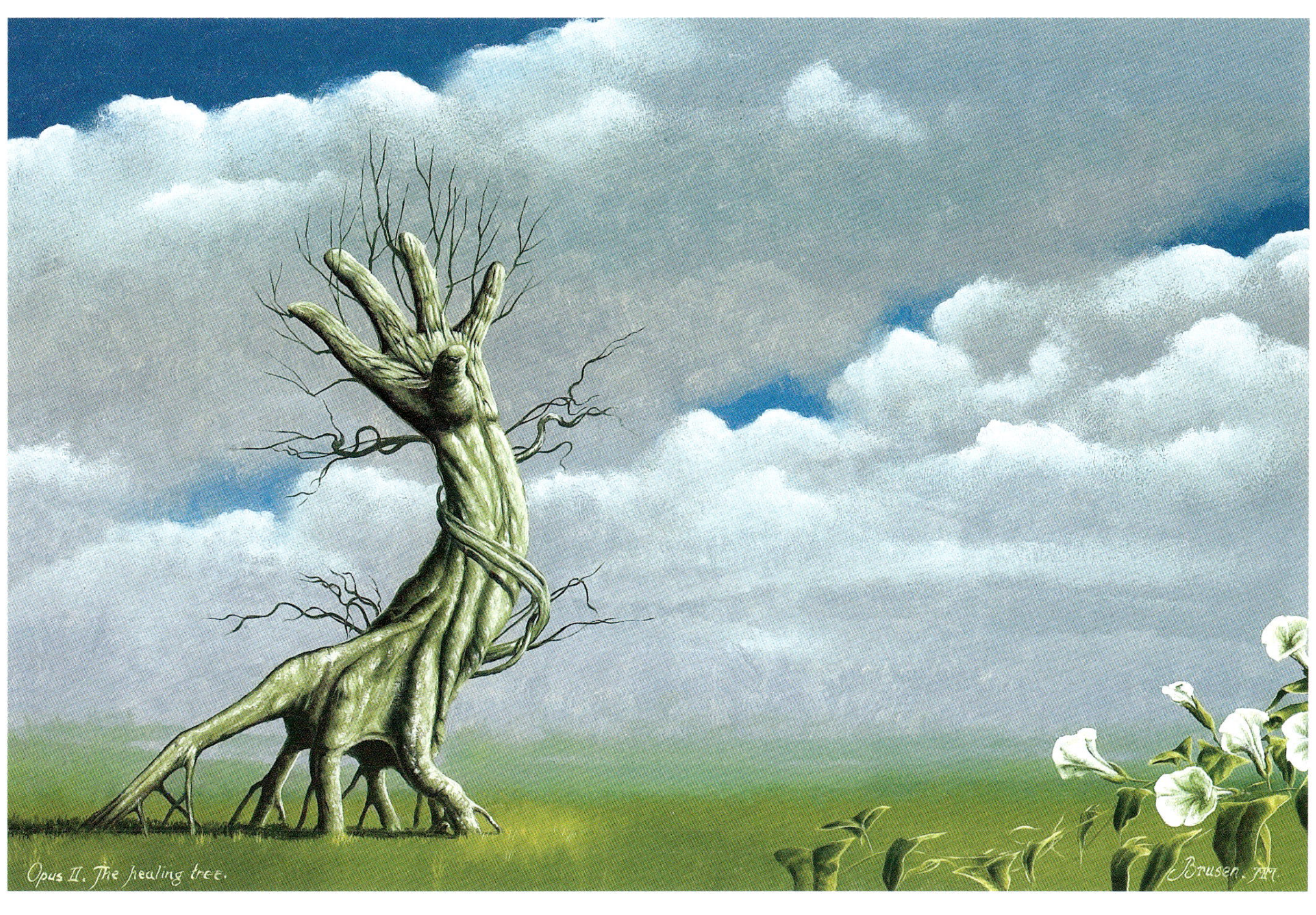
Opus II. The healing tree.
Brusen. MM.

∽ OPUS 6 ∼

Forest Playground

Oil on Wood • 40 x 60 cm • 2000

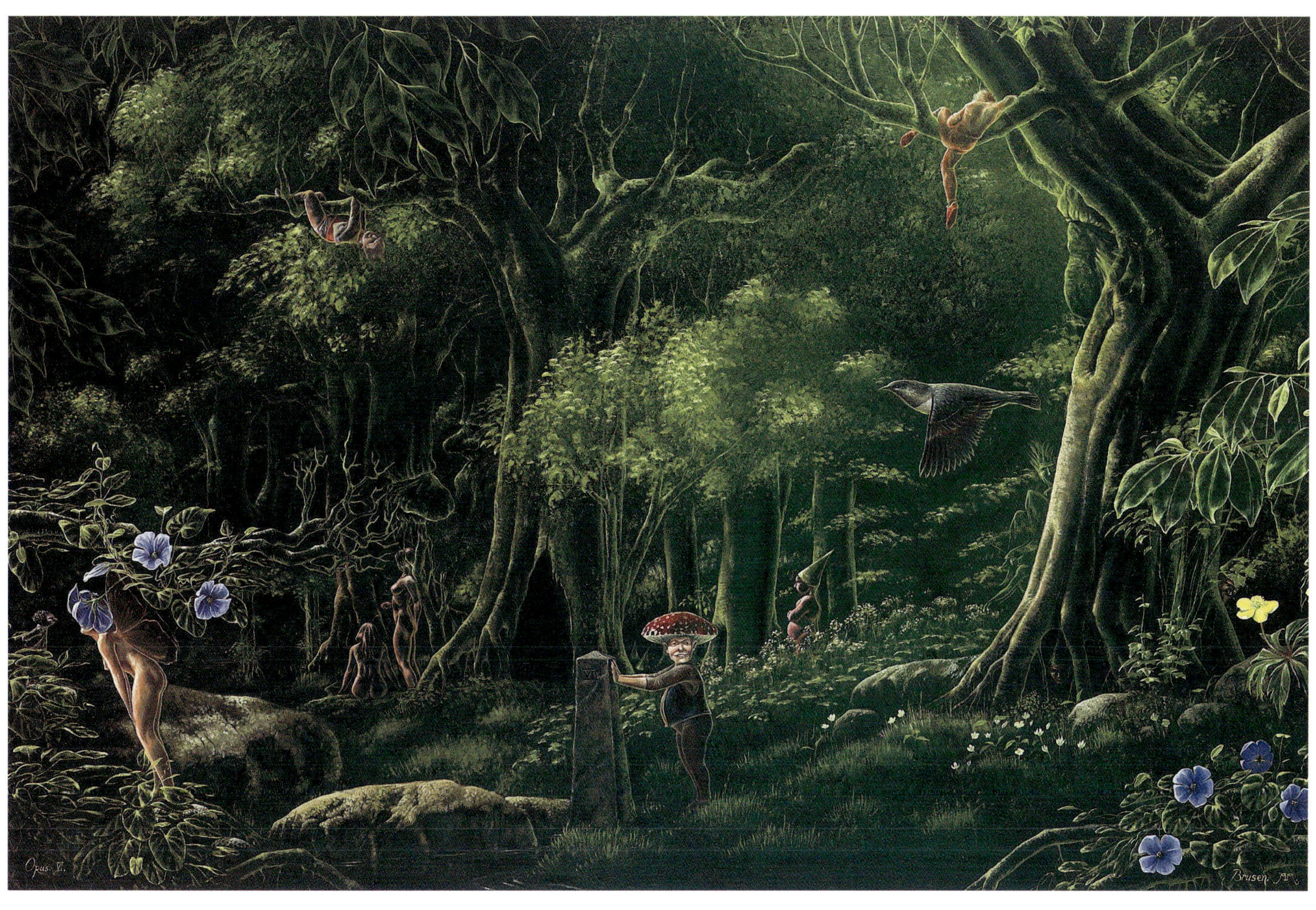

OPUS 7 & 8

Old Tree I & II

Both Oil on Wood • 20 x 15 cm • 2000

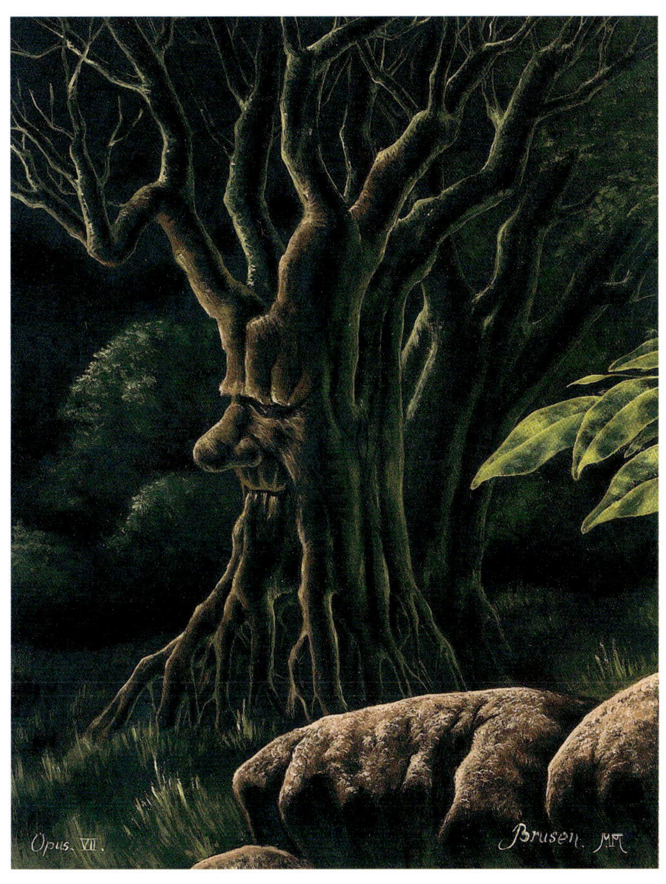
Opus. VII.
Brusen.

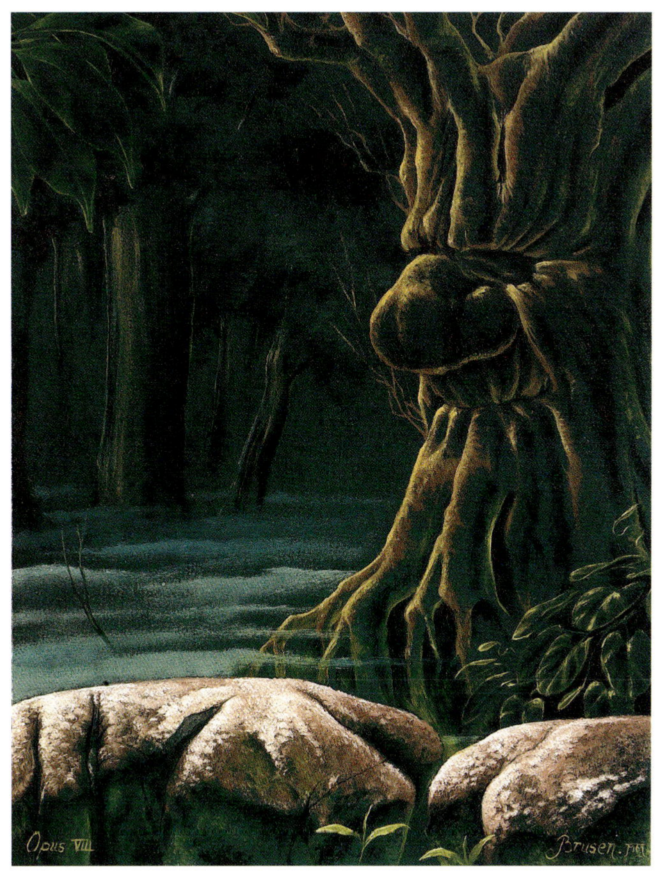
Opus VIII
Brusen.

OPUS 9

Magic Forest I

Oil on Wood • 40 x 30 cm • 2000

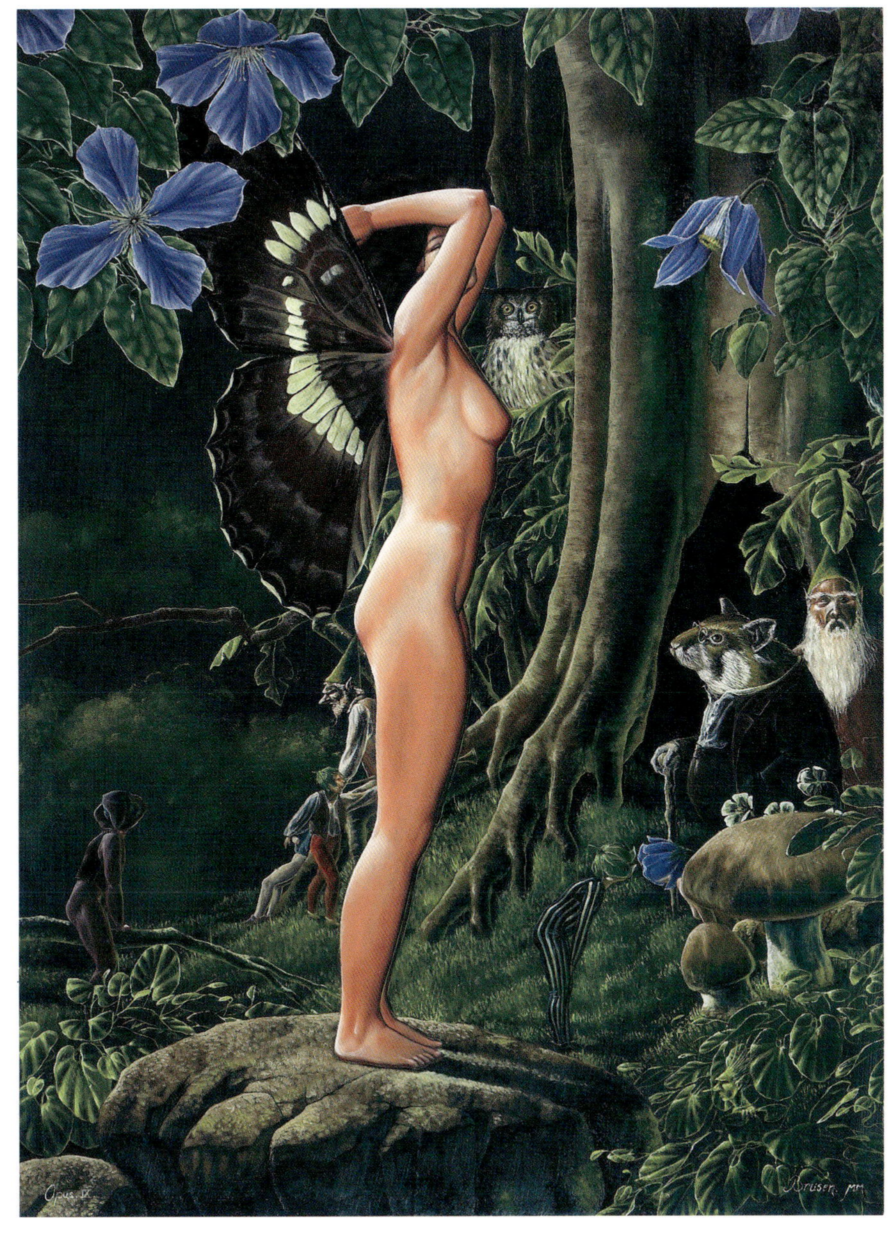
Opus. IX
Krusen. MM

OPUS 12

Tiny Fairy

Oil on Wood • 20 x 29 cm • 2000

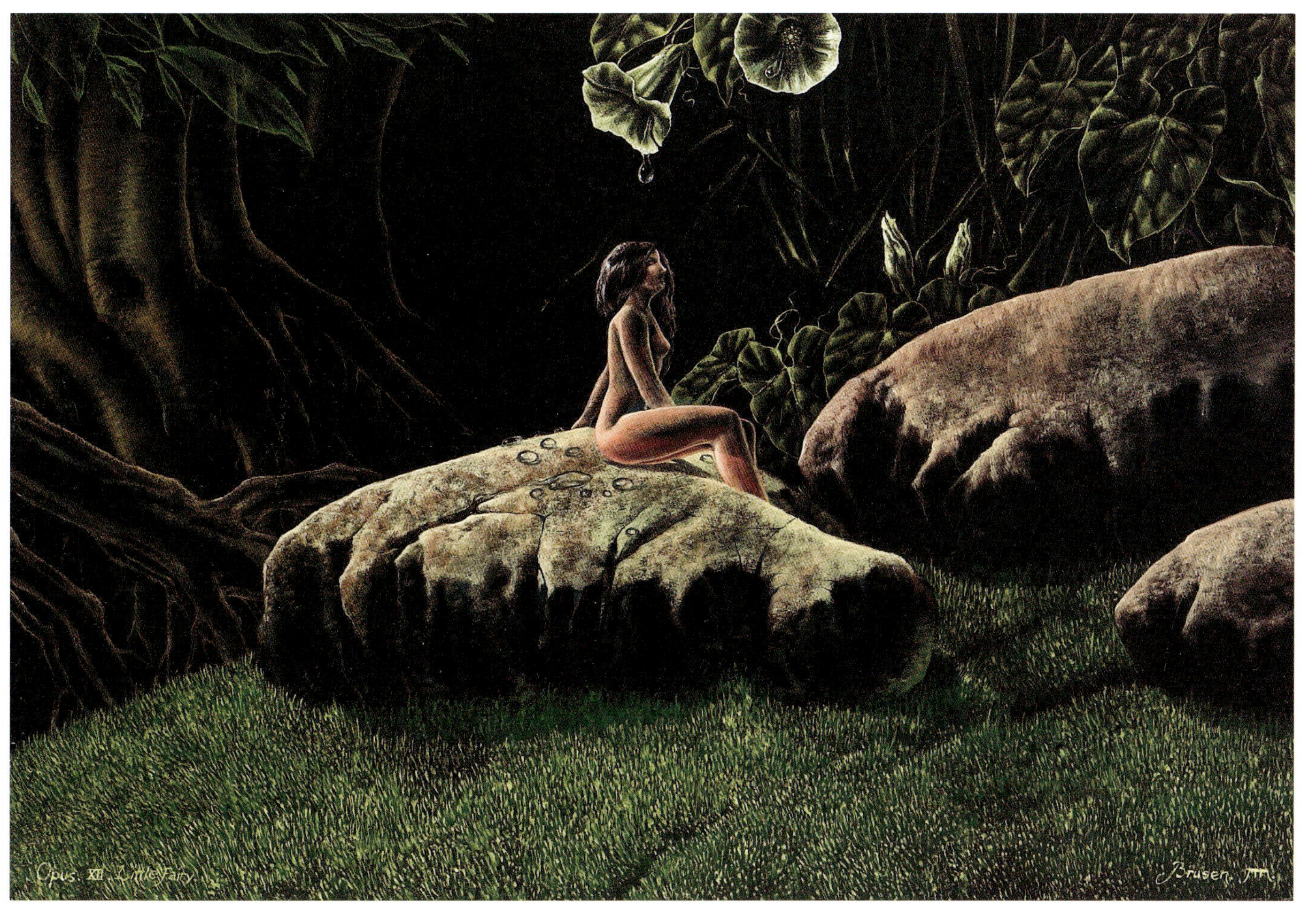
Opus. XII. Little Fairy.
Brusen.

OPUS 15

Sorrow

Oil on Wood • 30 x 40 cm • 2000

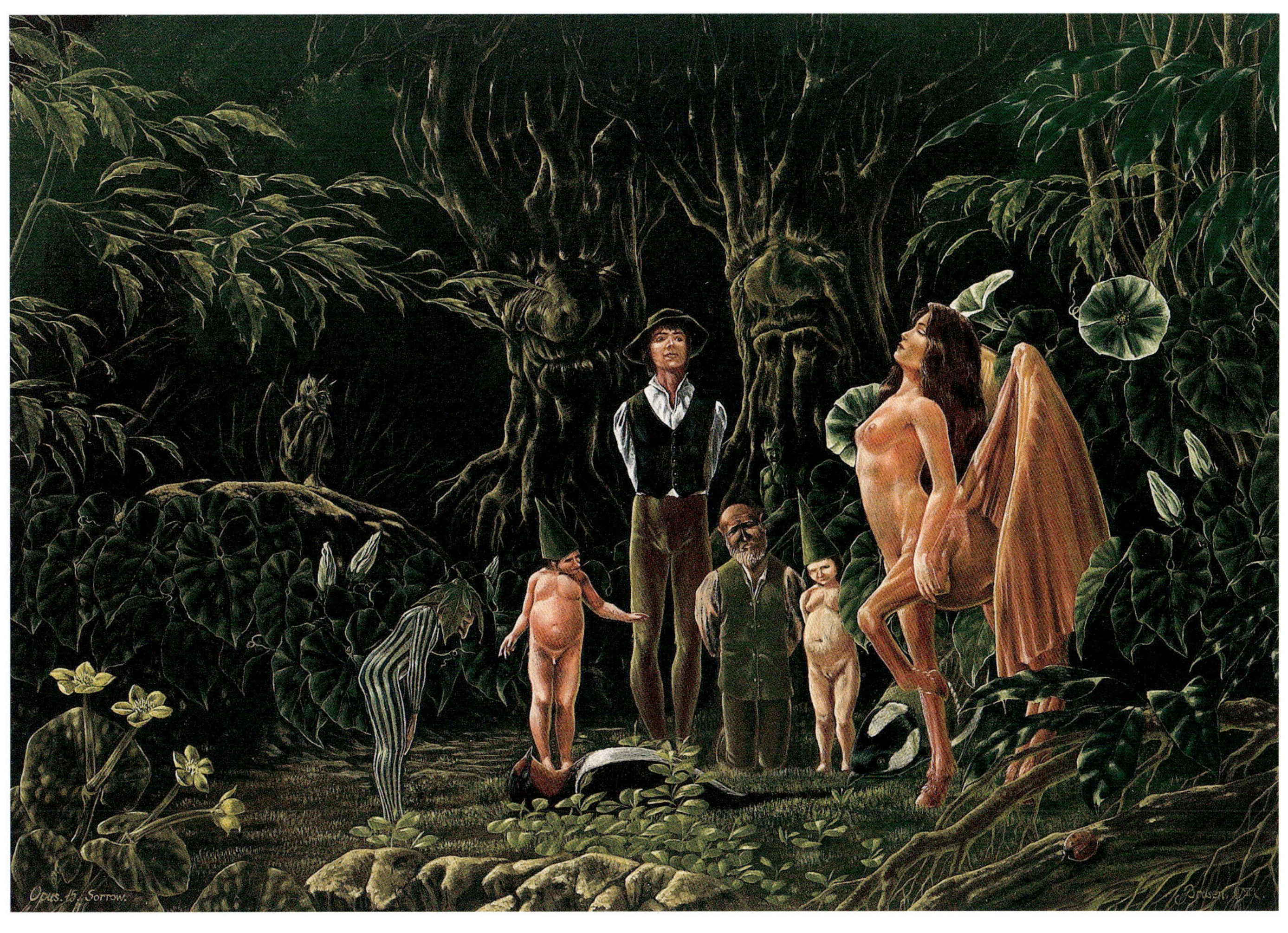
Opus. 15. Sorrow.

OPUS 20

Fairymasters Judgement

Oil on Wood • 40 x 60 cm • 2000

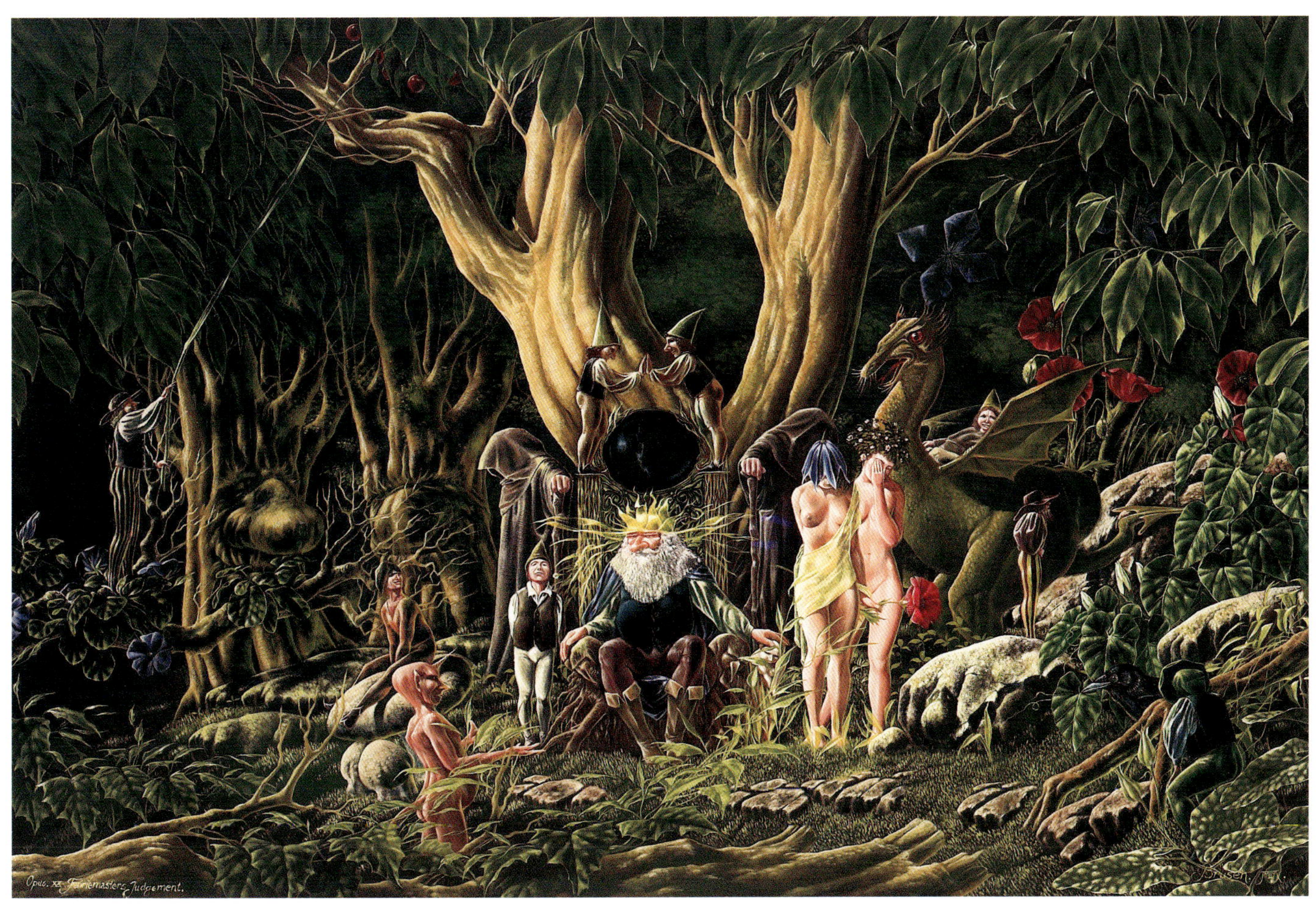
Opus. XX Fairiemasters Judgement.

~ OPUS 21 & 22 ~

Sleepwalker Oil on Wood • 20 x 15 cm • 2000
Music I Oil on Wood • 30 x 20 cm • 2000

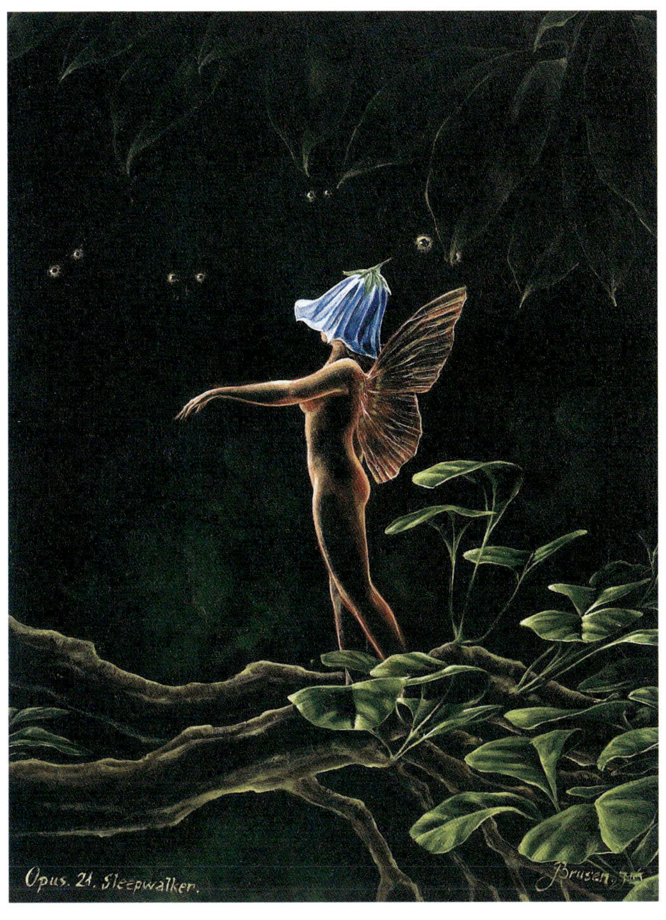
Opus. 21. Sleepwalker.
Brusen.

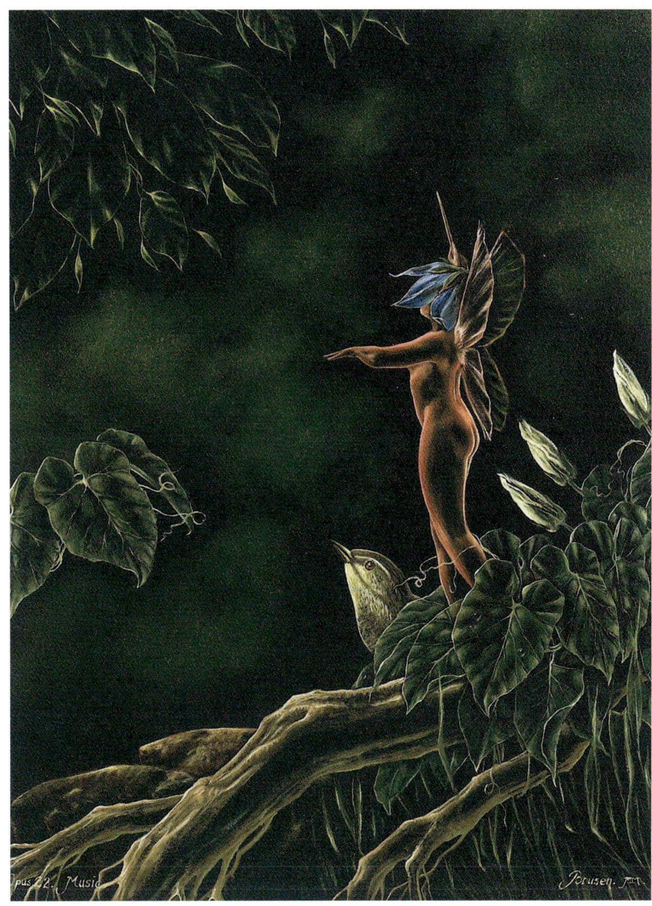
pus 22. Music
Brusen.

OPUS 25

Love

Oil on Wood • 28 x 31 cm • 2000

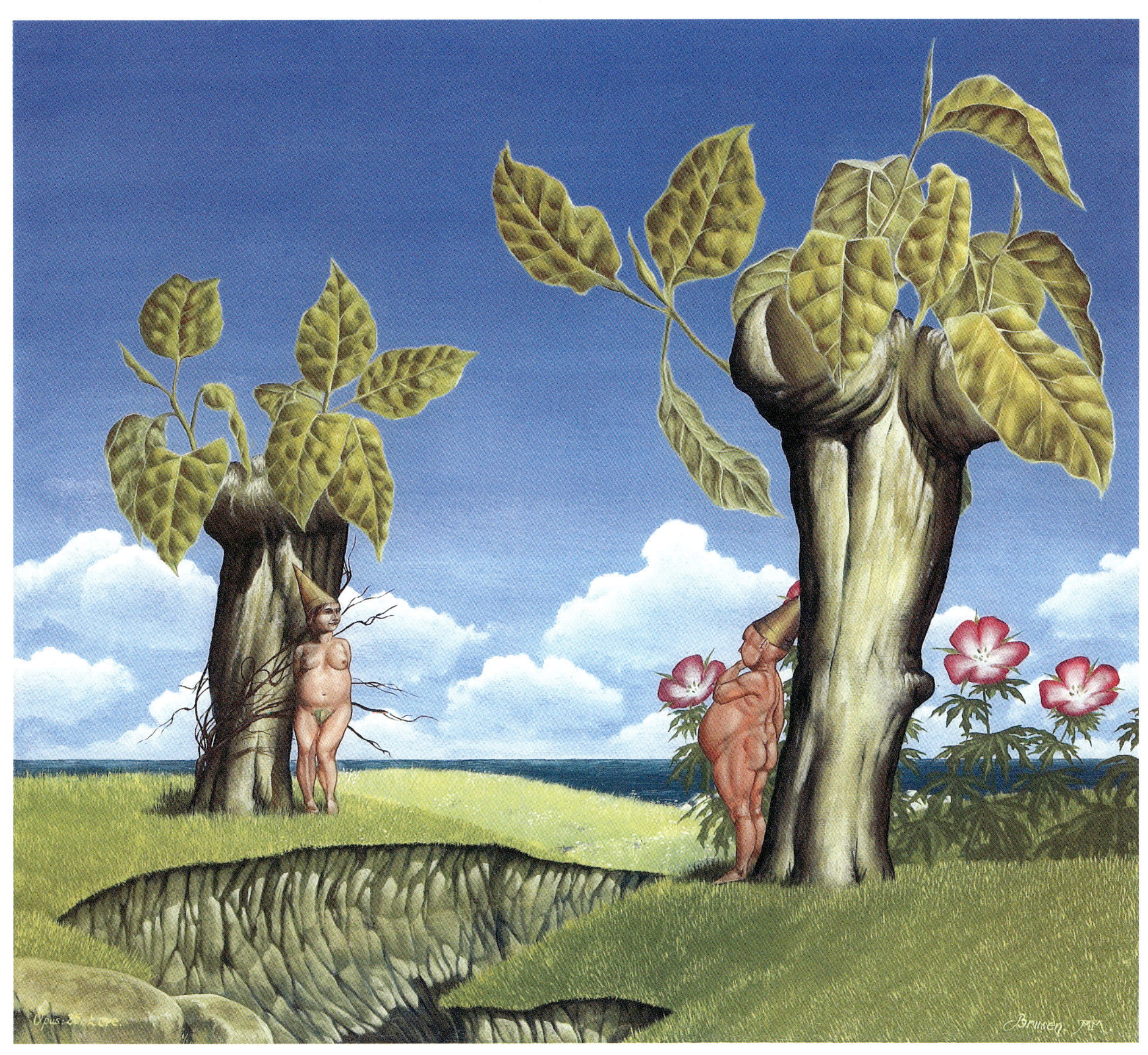

OPUS 28

The Boy and the Dragon

Oil on Wood • 30 x 45 cm • 2000

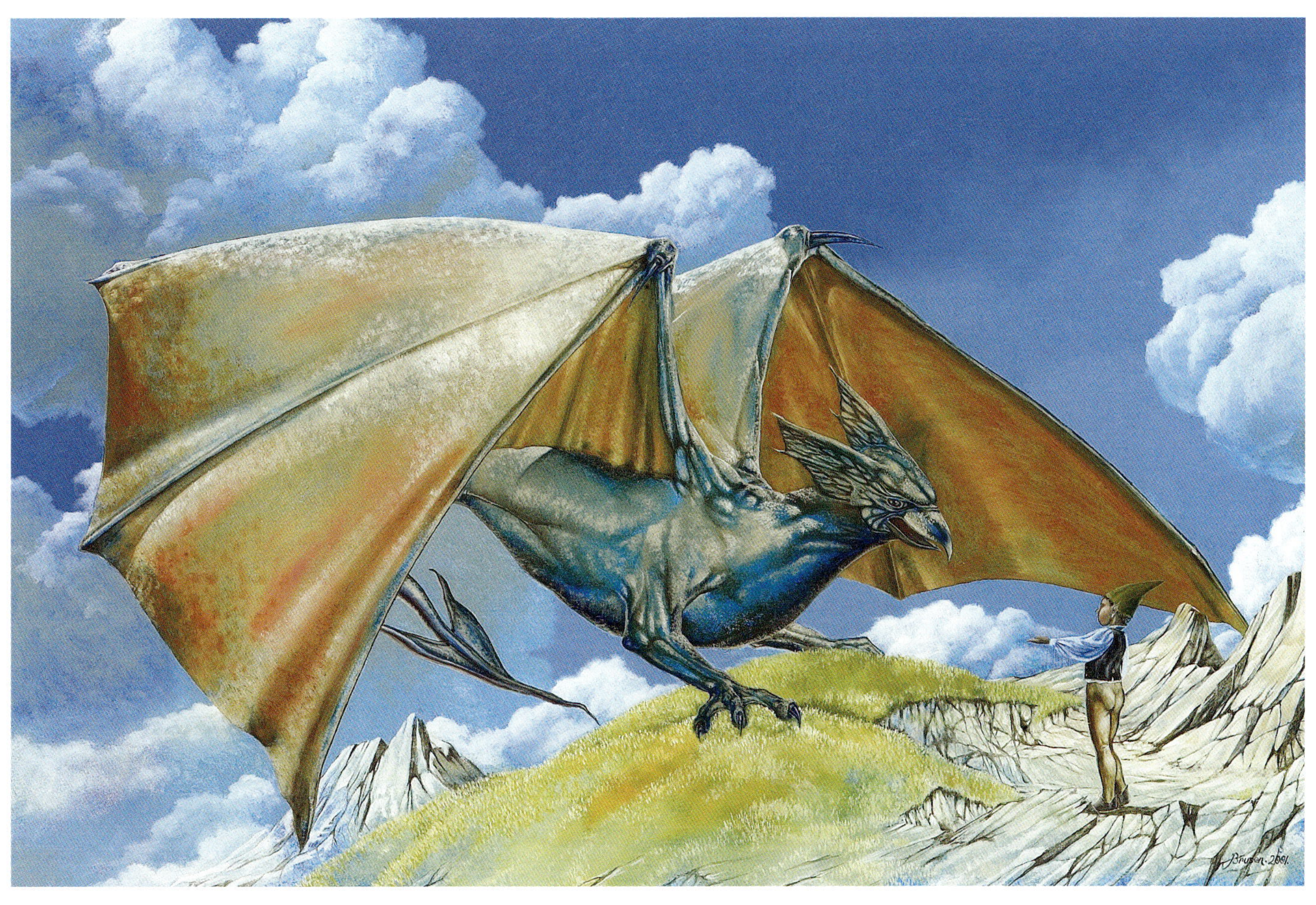

∽ OPUS 34 ∼

Bug

Oil on Wood •20 x 16 cm • 2001

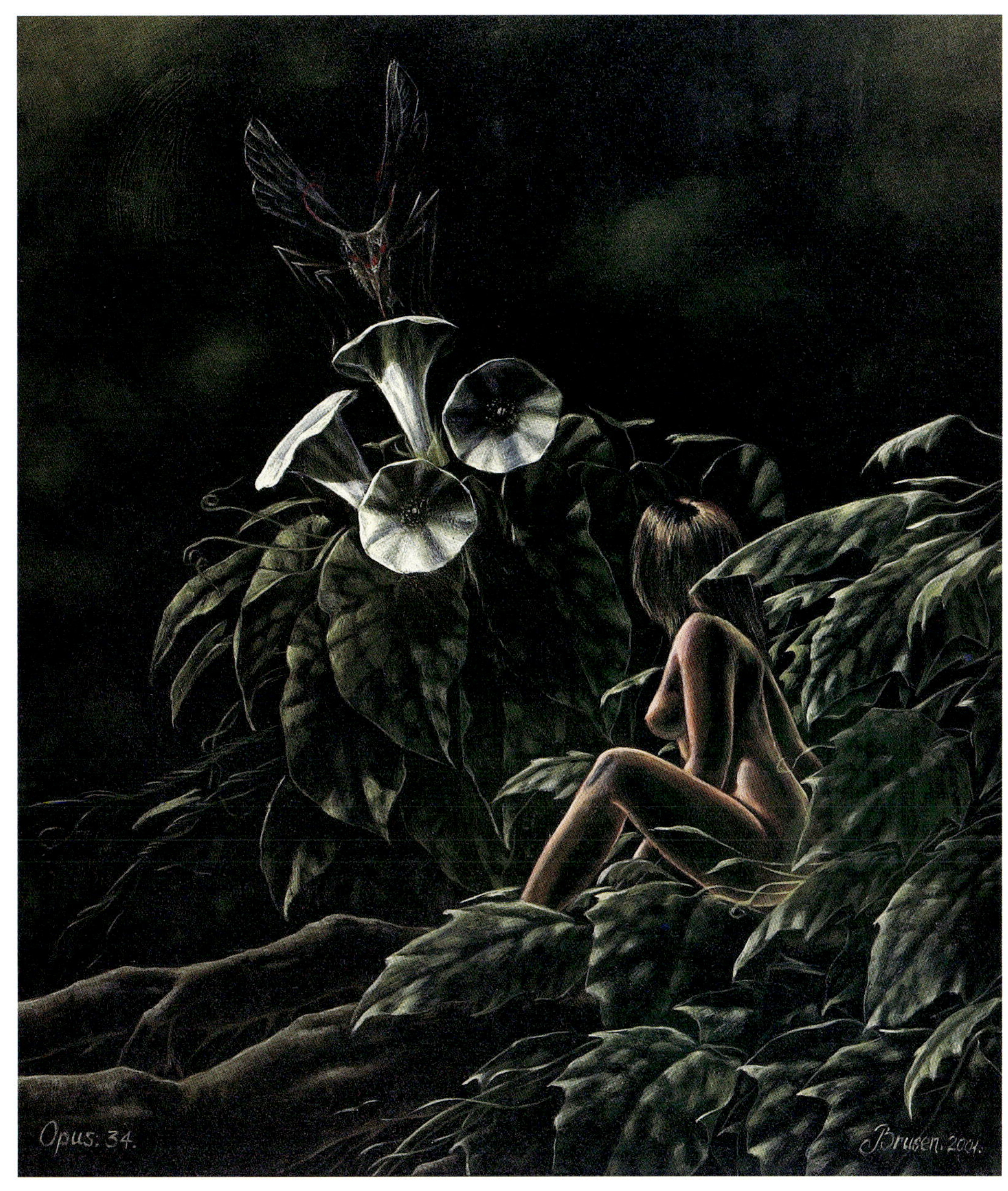
Opus. 34.
Brusen. 2004.

OPUS 35

No Title

Oil on Wood • 20 x 30 cm • 2001

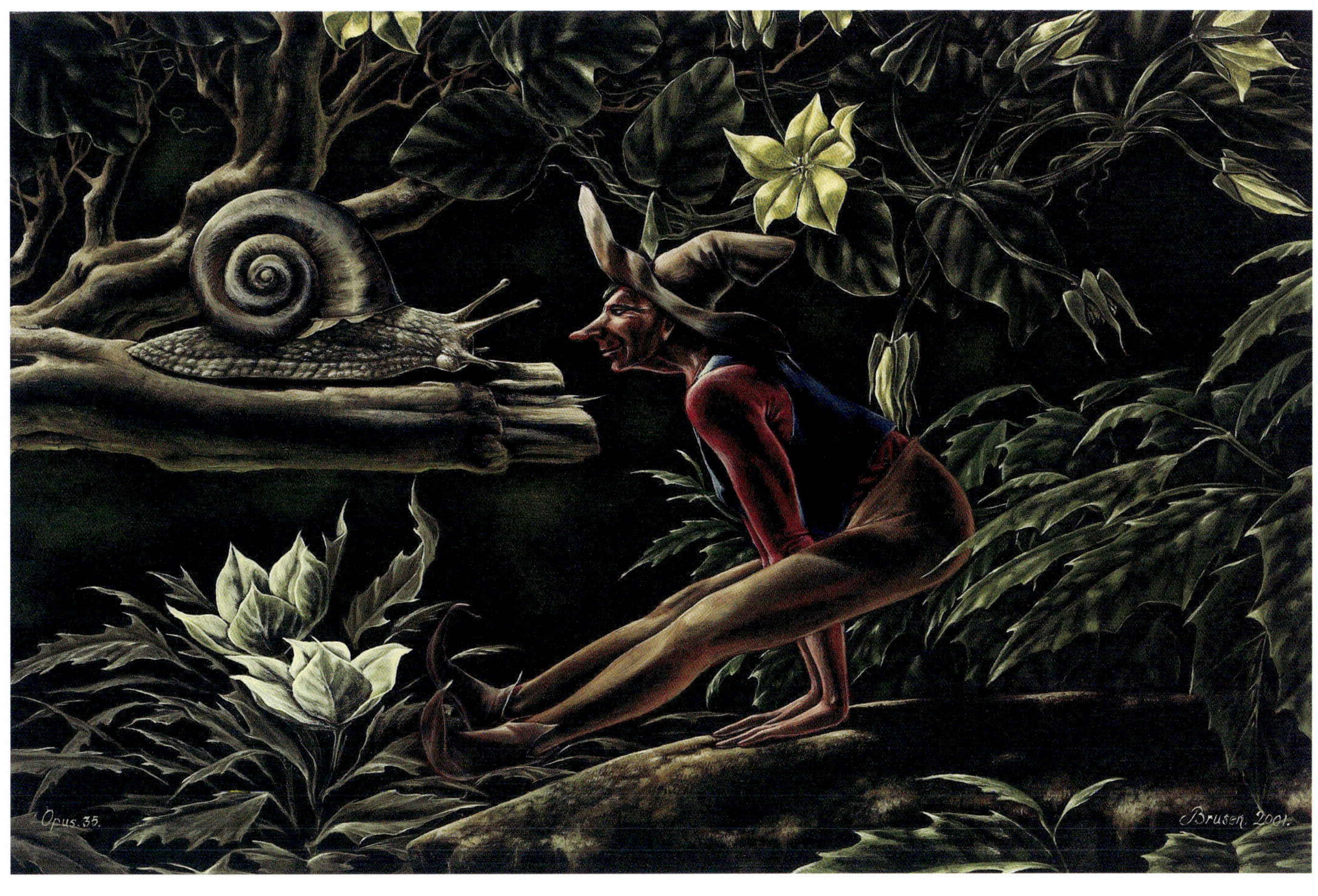
Opus. 35.
Brusen 2001.

OPUS 37

The Splash

Oil on Wood • 20 x 16 cm • 2001

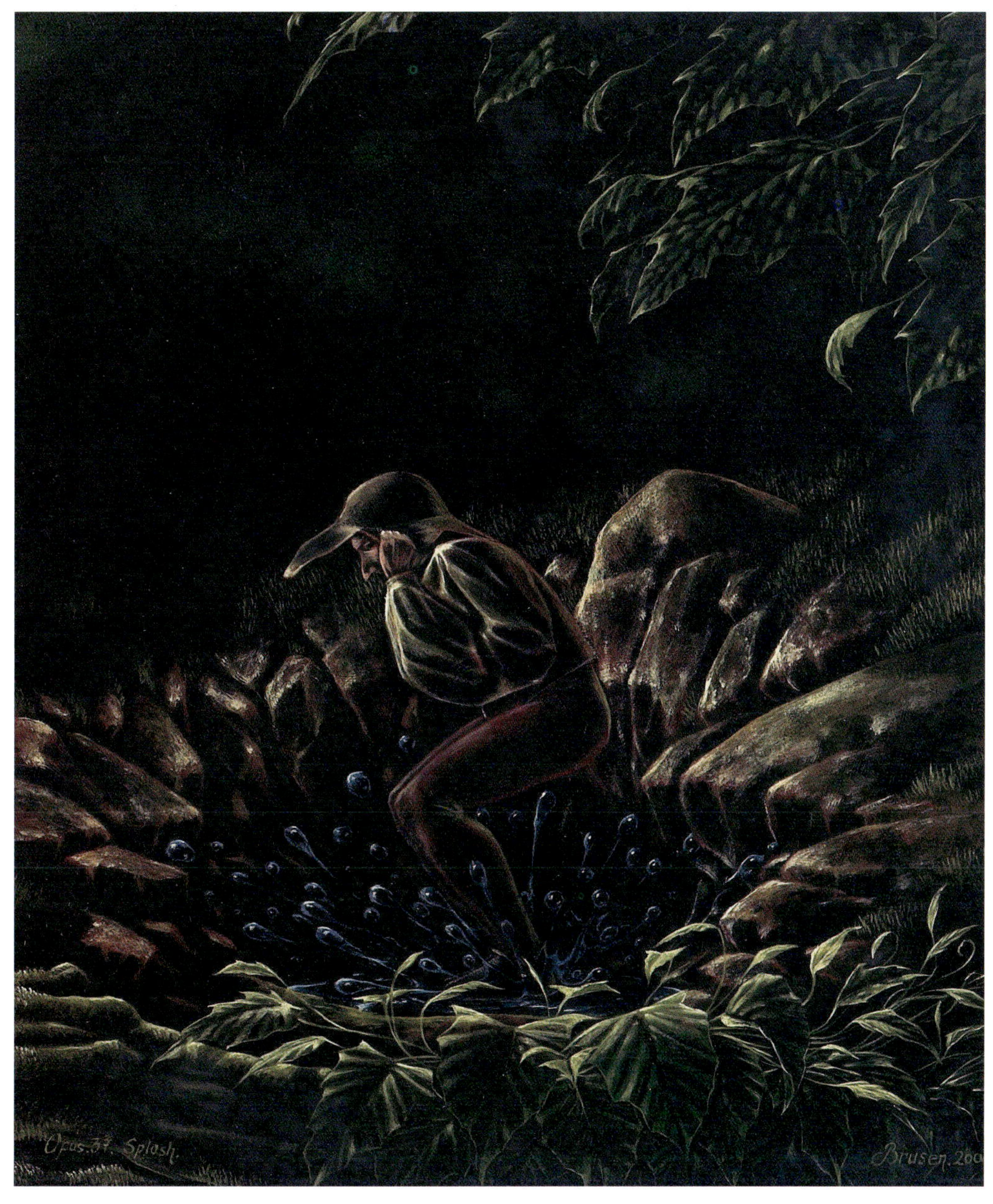
Opus.37. Splosh.
Brusen.200

∽ OPUS 41 ∾

The Joymaster

Oil on Wood • 20 x 16 cm • 2001

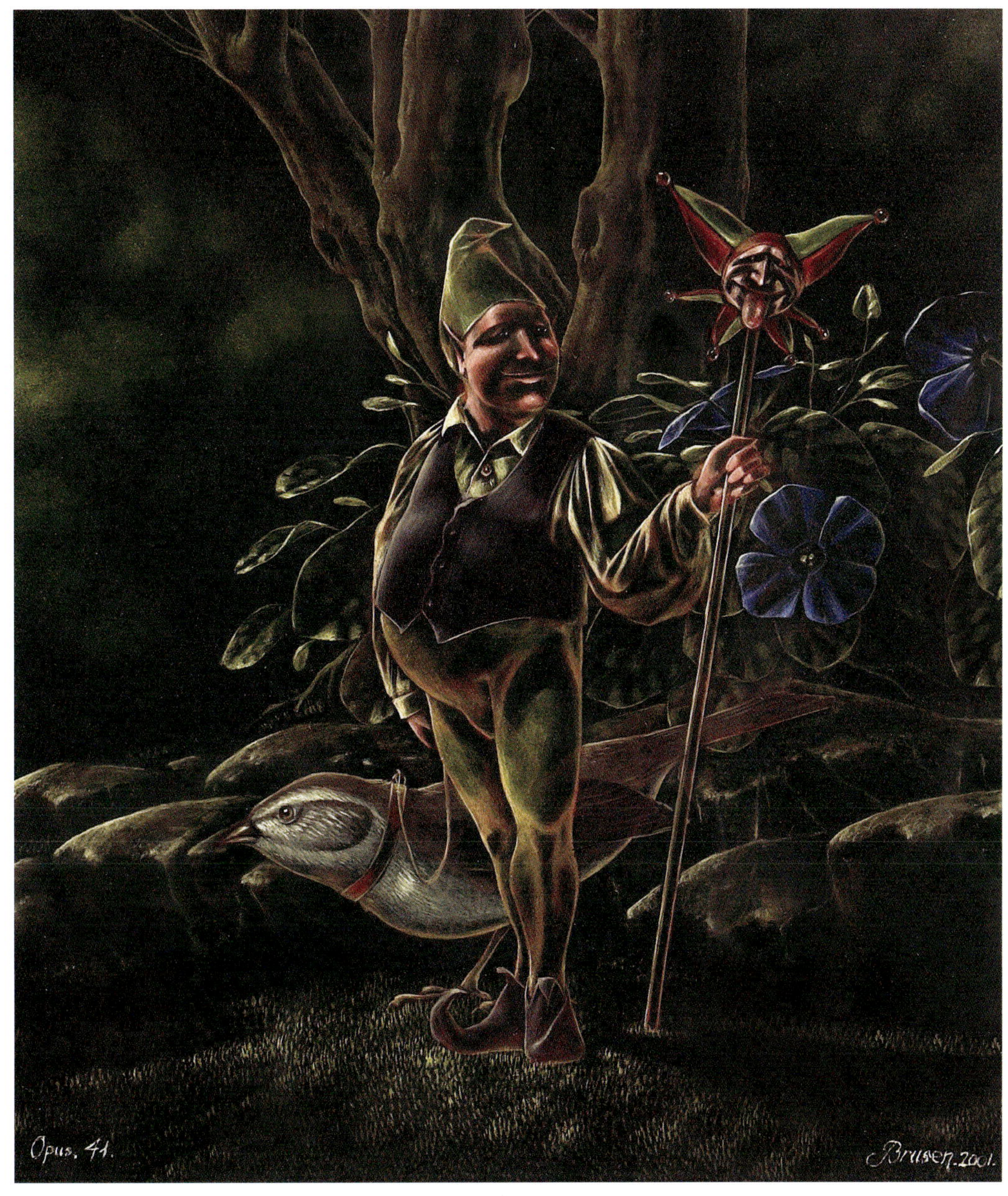
Opus. 41.
Brusen.2001.

OPUS 43

Sweet as Honey

Oil on Wood • 40 x 60 cm • 2001

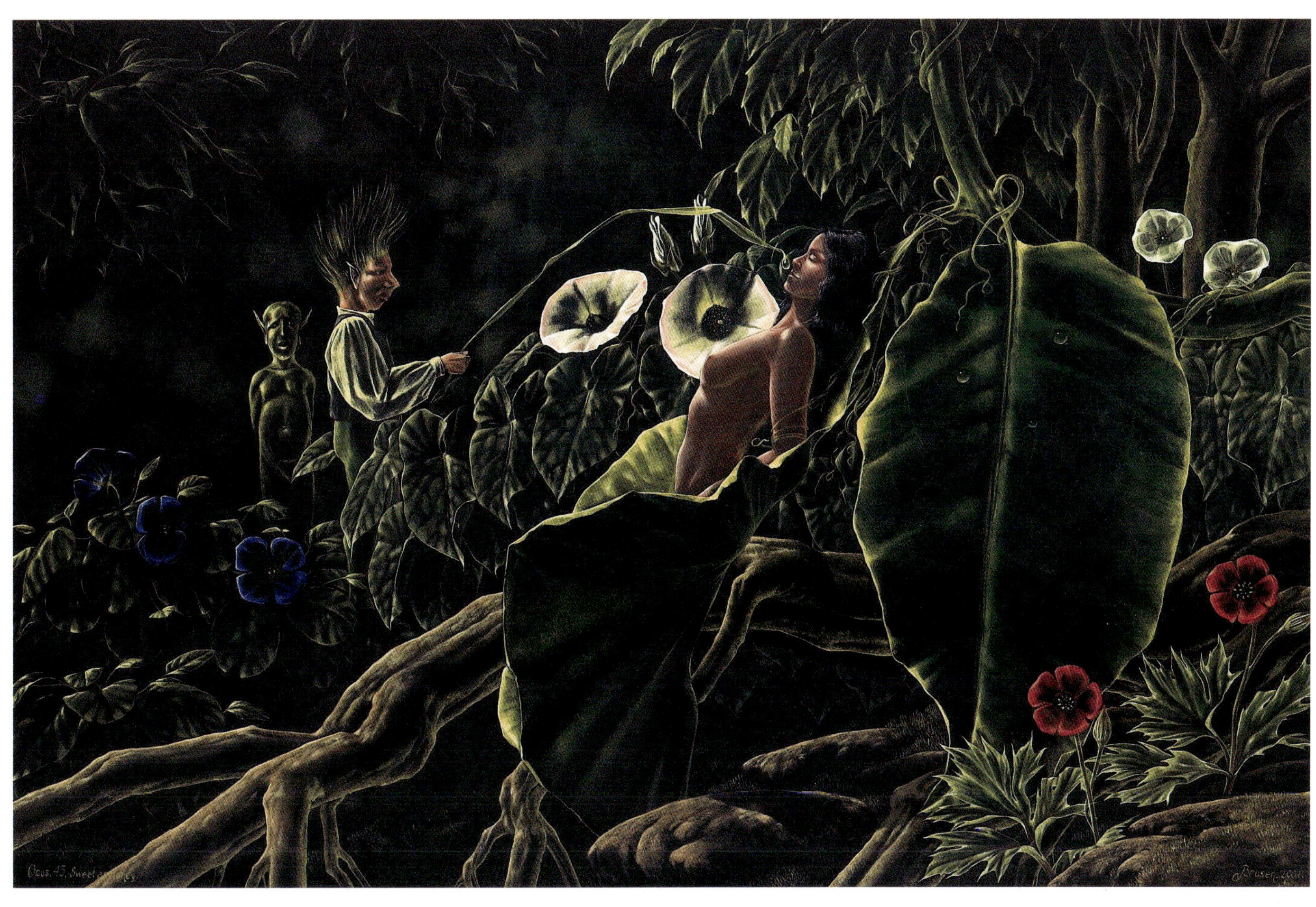
Opus. 45. Sweet
Brusen

∽ OPUS 44 ∾

Alf

Oil on Wood • 30 x 20 cm • 2001

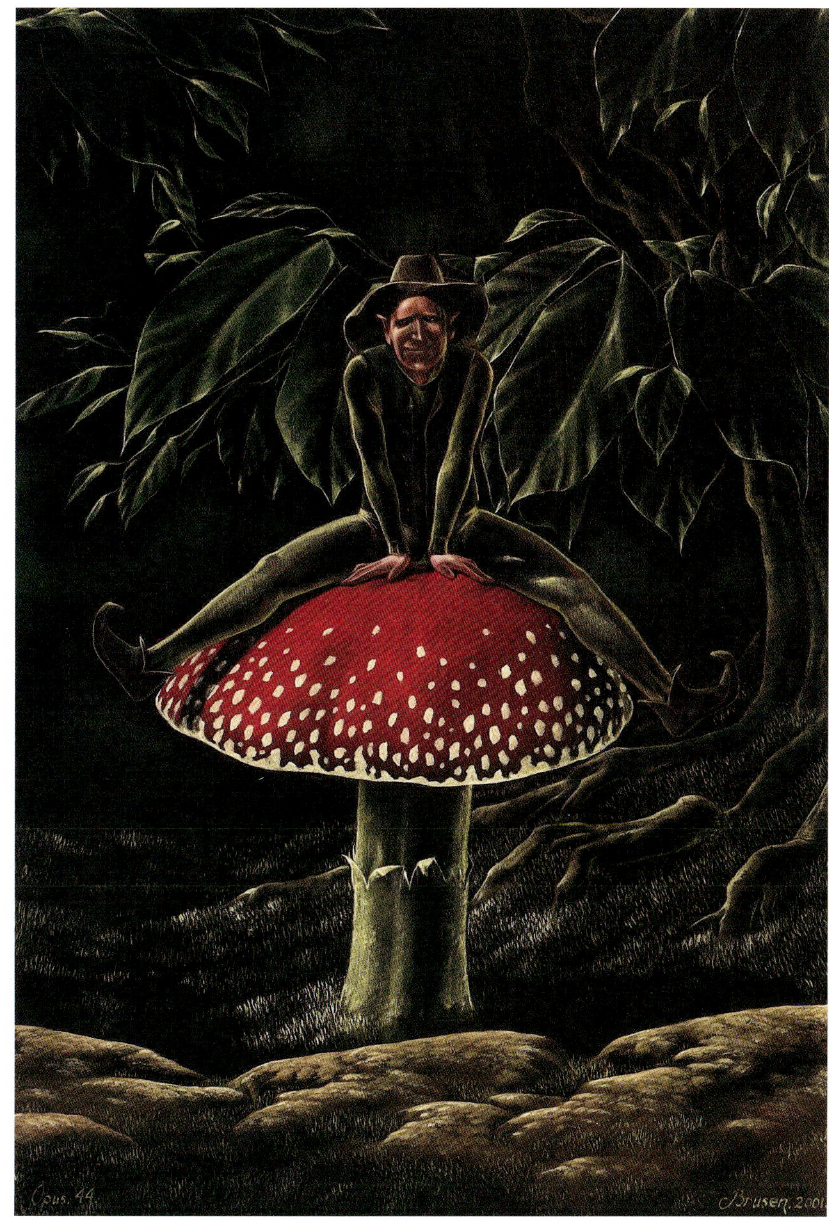
Opus. 44
Brusen. 2001

OPUS45

Spirit of the lake

Oil on Wood • 16 x 20 cm • 2001

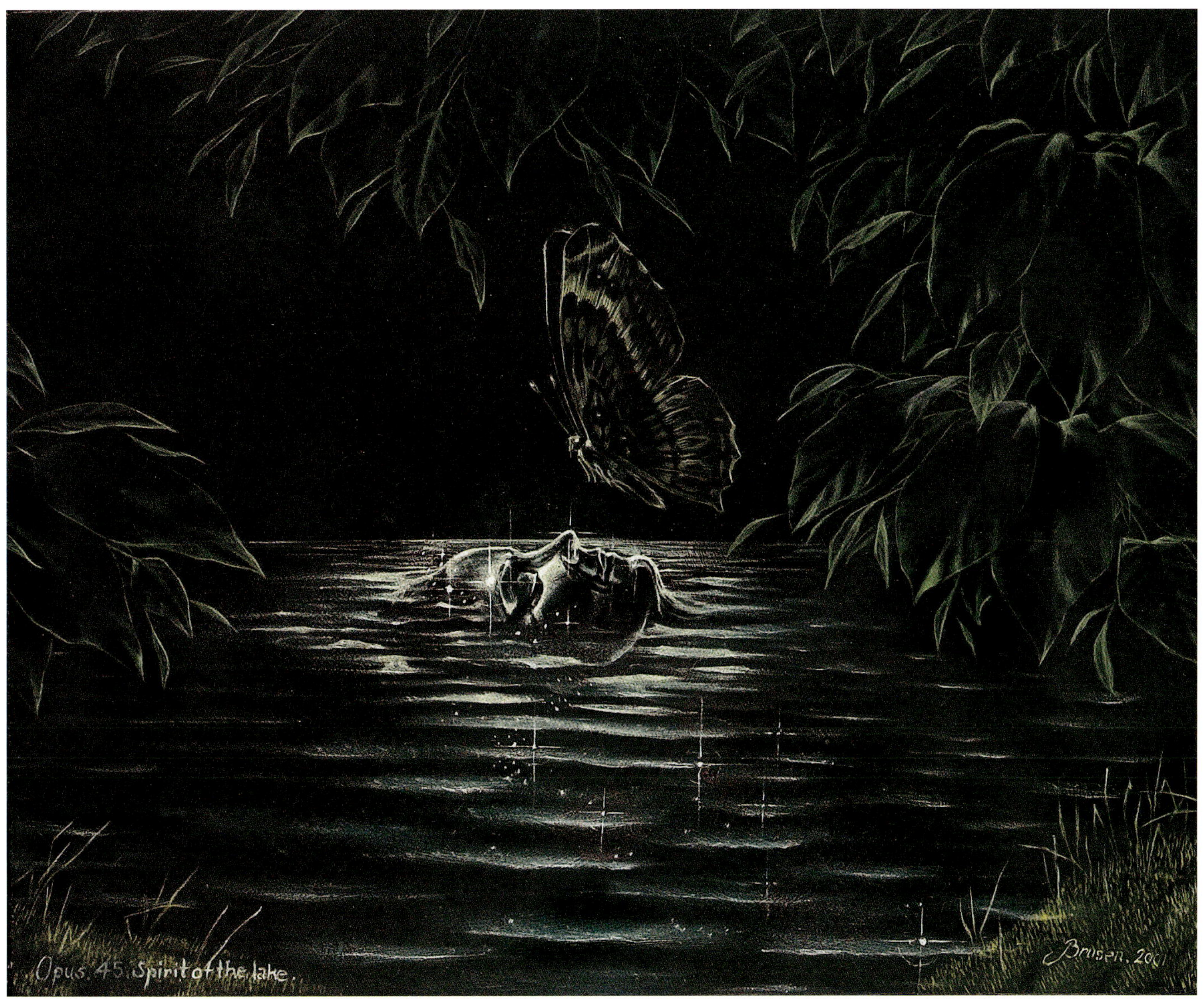
Opus. 45. Spirit of the lake.
Brusen. 2001

OPUS 47

Don't play with my food

Oil on Wood • 80 x 60 cm • 2001

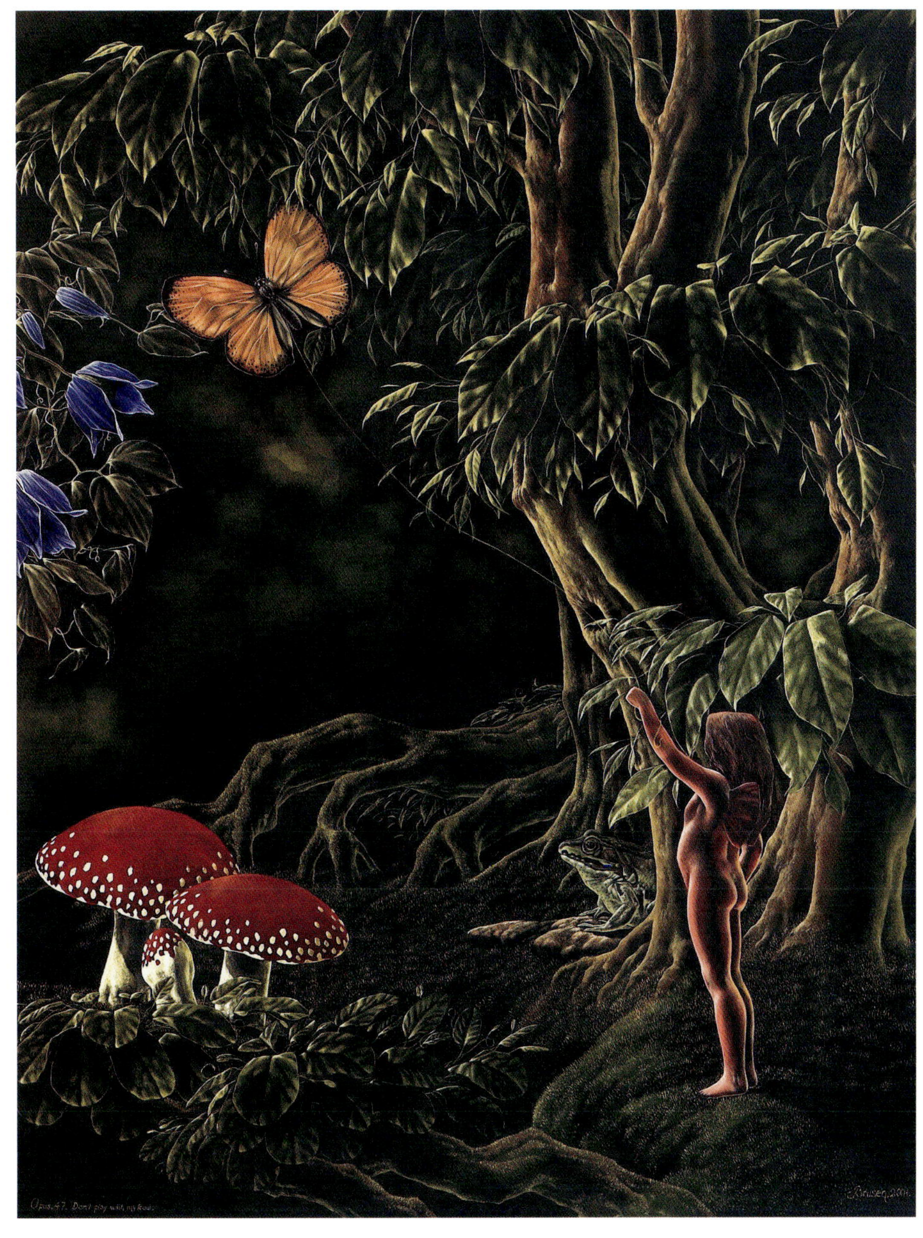
Opus.47. Dont play with my toad.

OPUS 49

The Finding

Oil on Wood • 80 x 120 cm • 2001

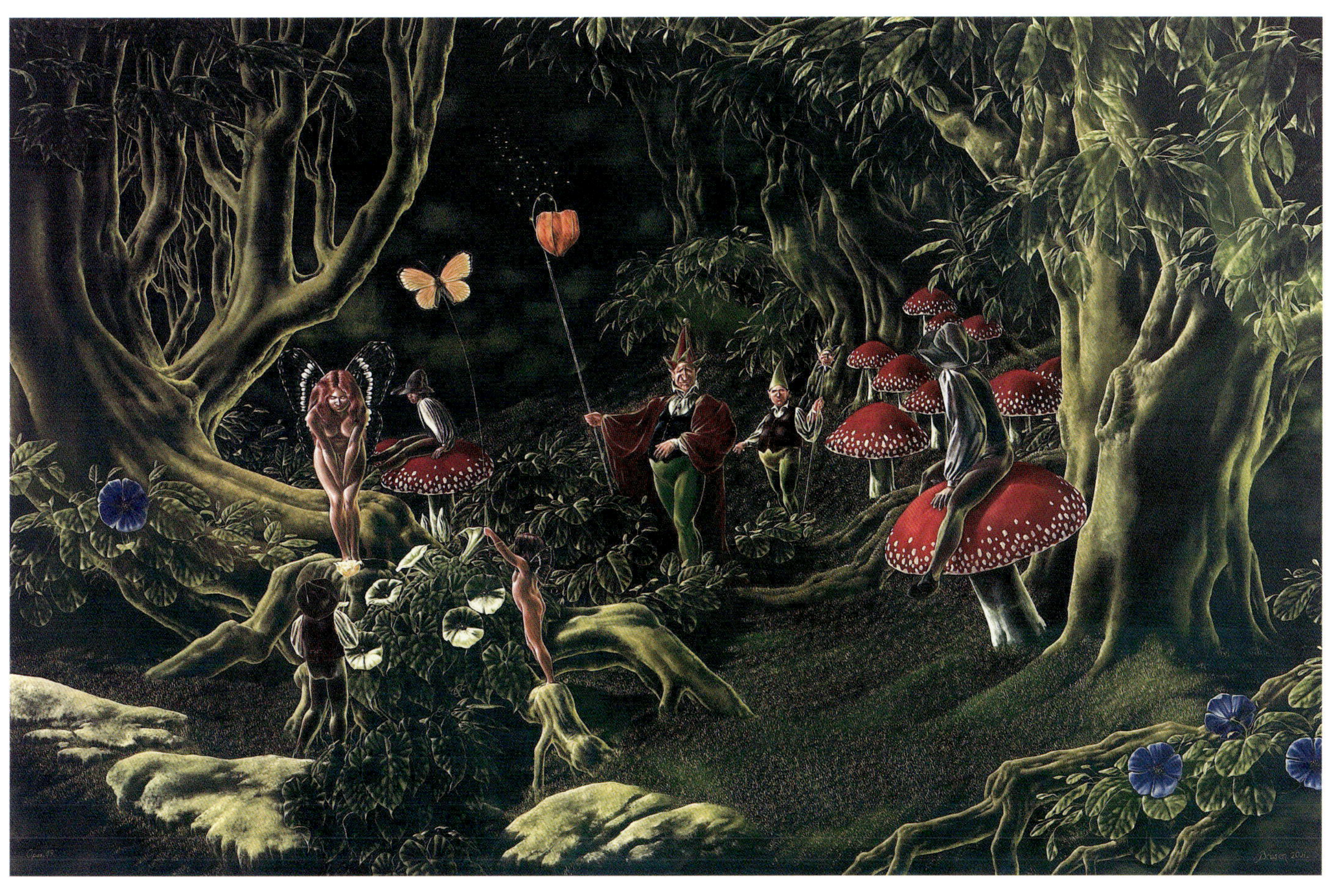

OPUS 52

Teasing

Oil on Wood • 40 x 60 cm • 2001

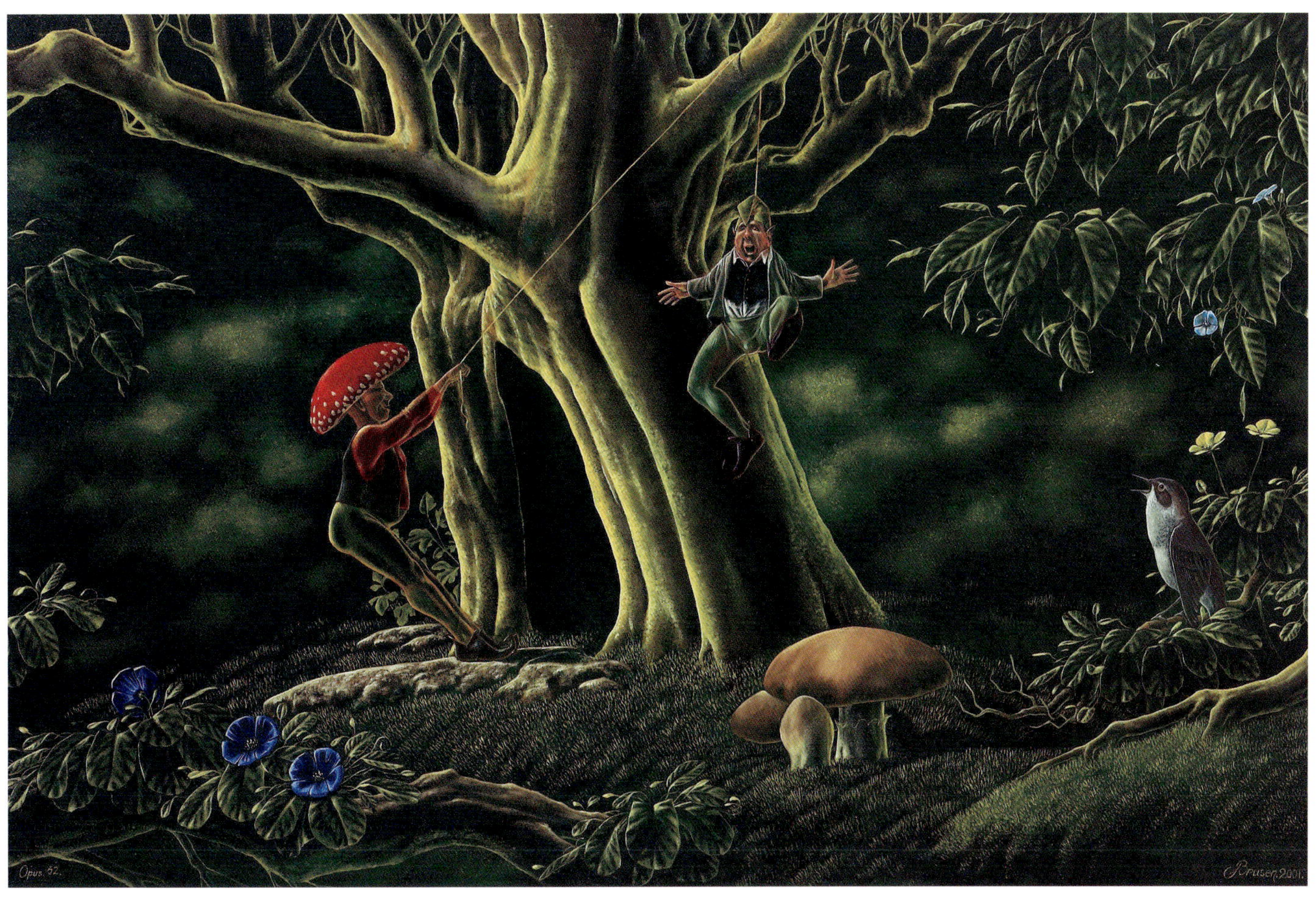
Opus. 62.
Brusen. 2001.

OPUS 62

Free and Flying

Oil on Wood • 20 x 15 cm • 2002

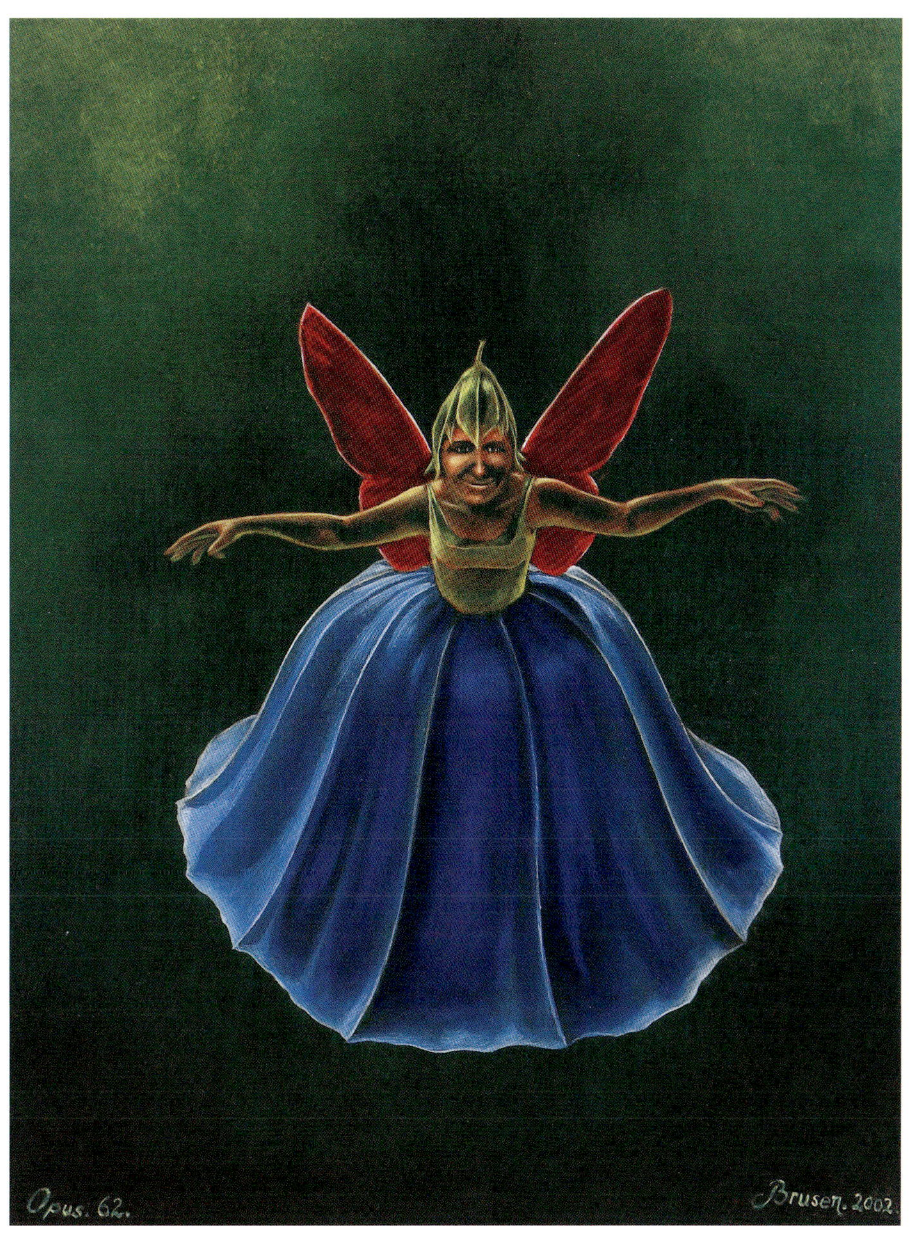
Opus. 62.
Brusen. 2002.

OPUS 84

Yellow Bird

Oil on Wood • 75 x 60 cm • 2002

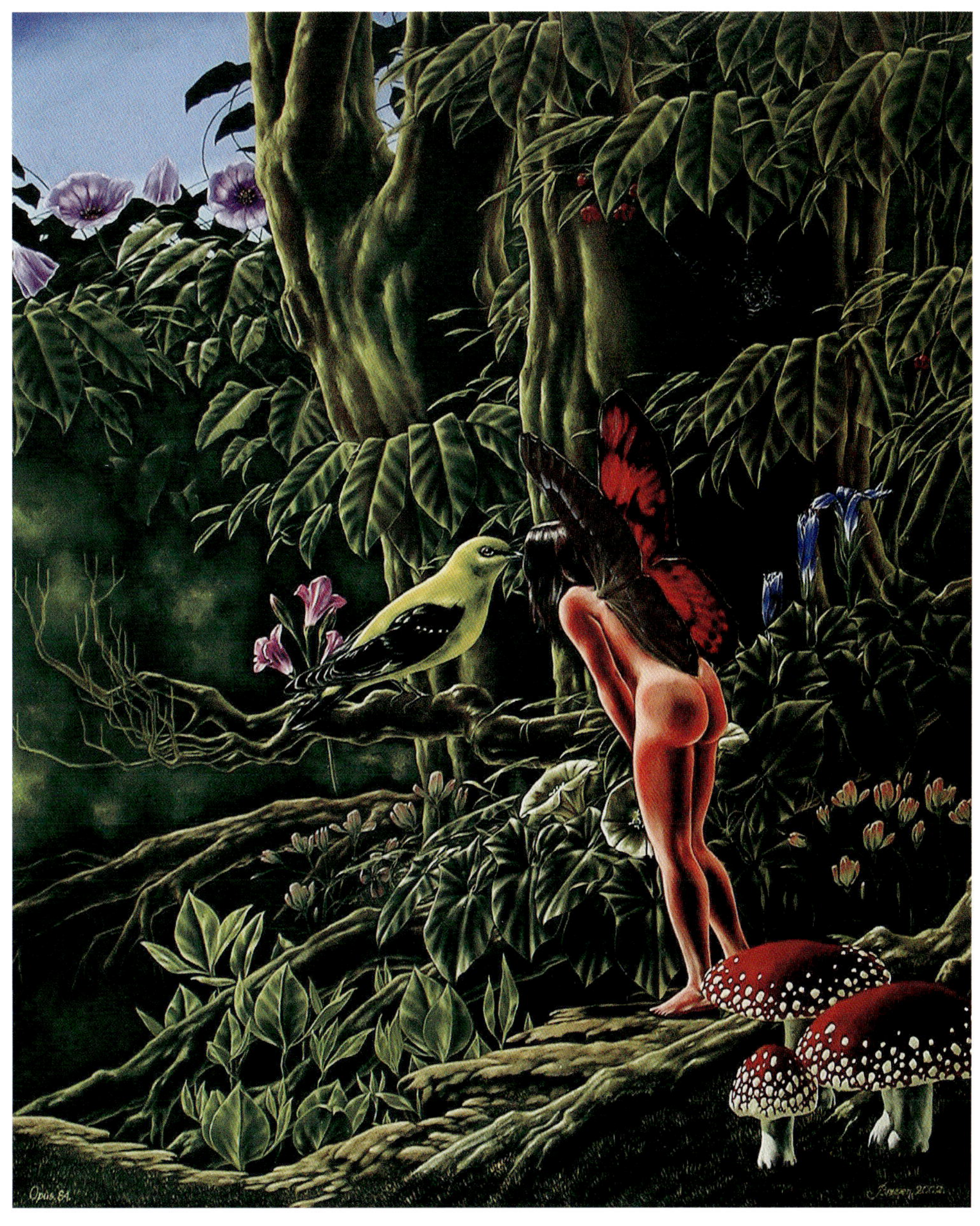

OPUS 88

Little Joe

Oil on Wood • 20 x 15 cm • 2002

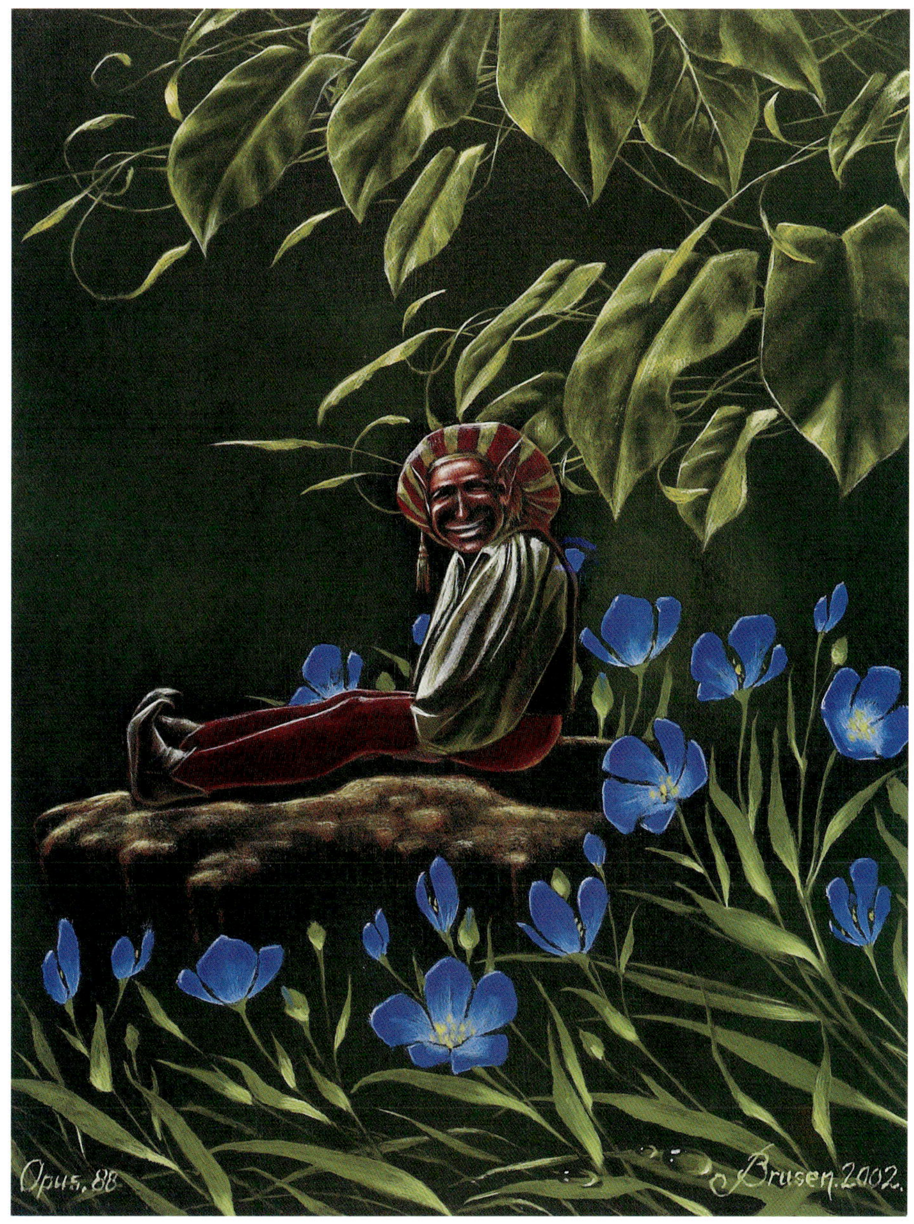
Opus. 88
Brusen. 2002.

OPUS 89

Land of Make Believe

Oil on Wood • 20 x 30 cm • 2002

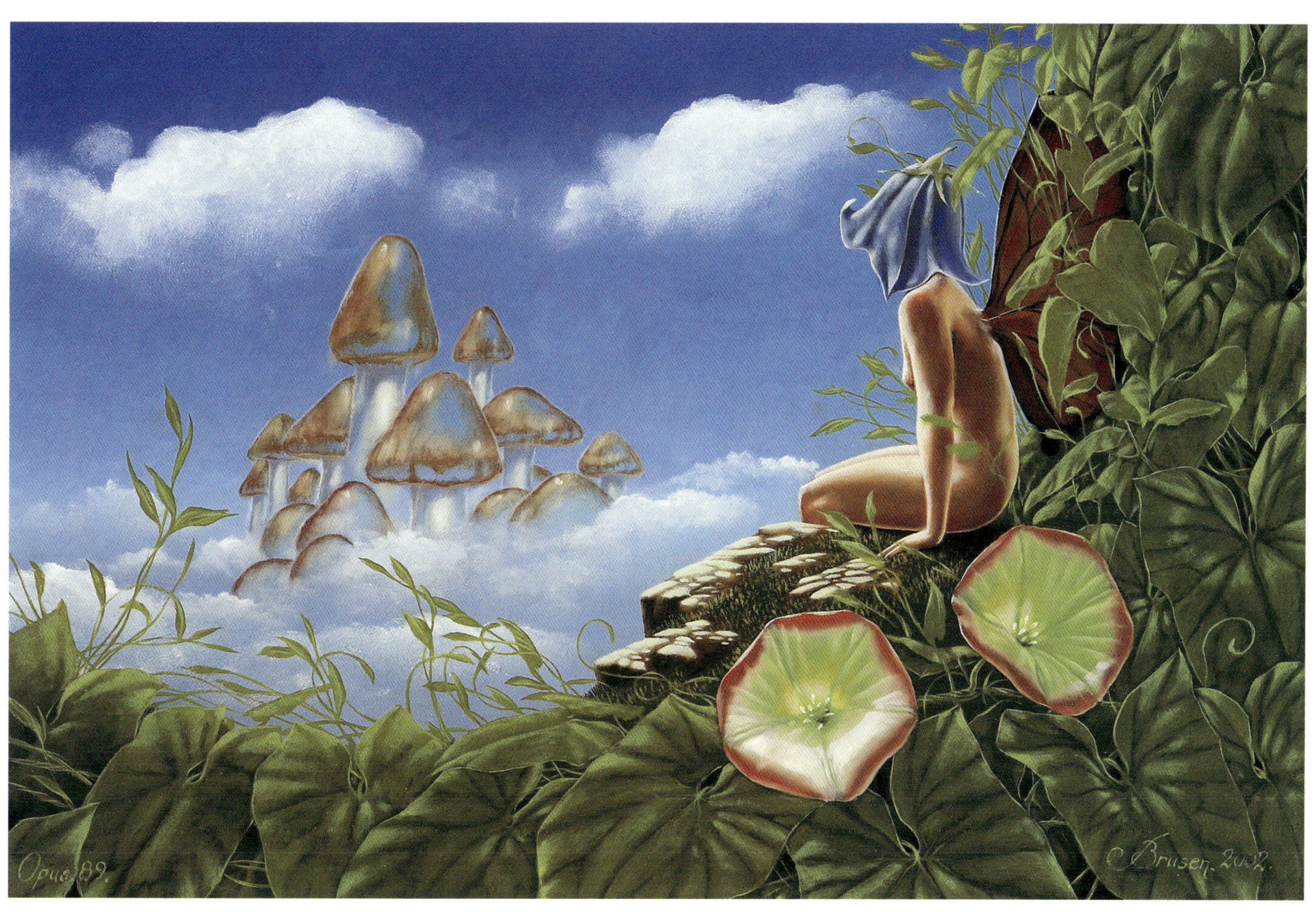
Opus 89.
© Brusen 2002.

OPUS 91

Gnome from Deep Forest

Oil on Wood • 30 x 20 cm • 2002

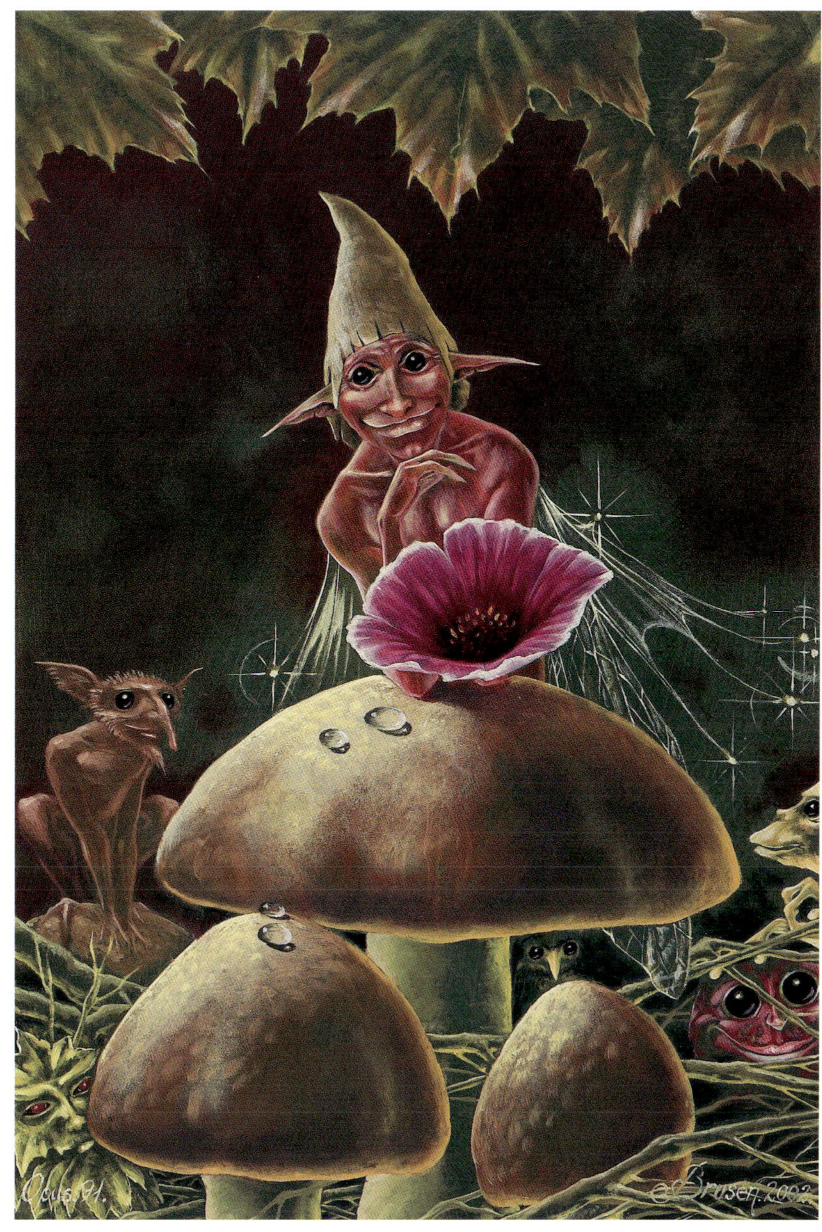

OPUS 93

Little Magic (triptych)

Oil on Wood • 45 x 80 cm *including frame* • 2003

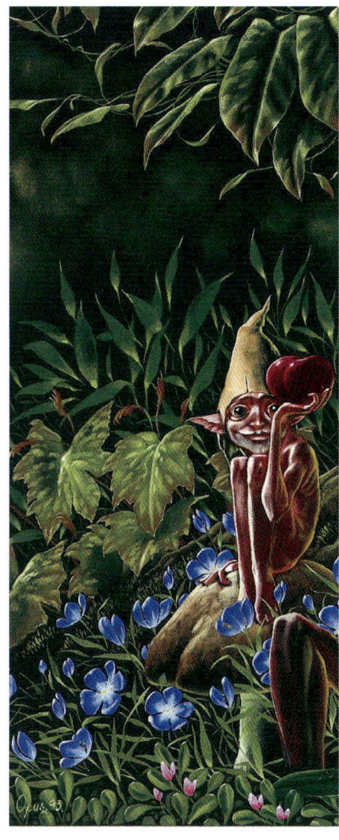

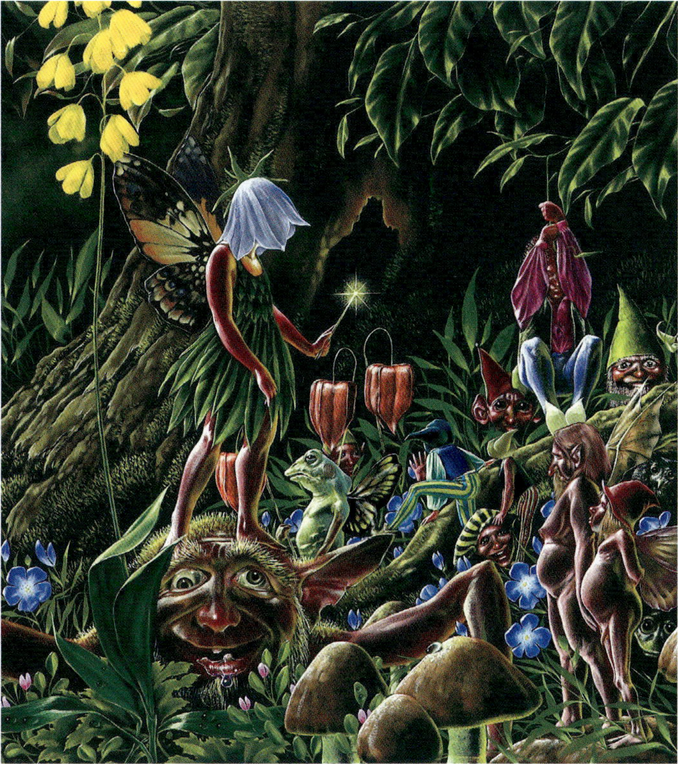

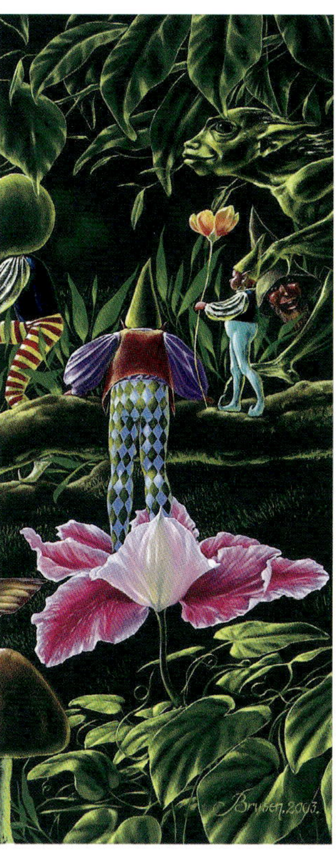

OPUS 96

A Flower Fairy

Oil on Wood • 35 x 30 cm • 2003

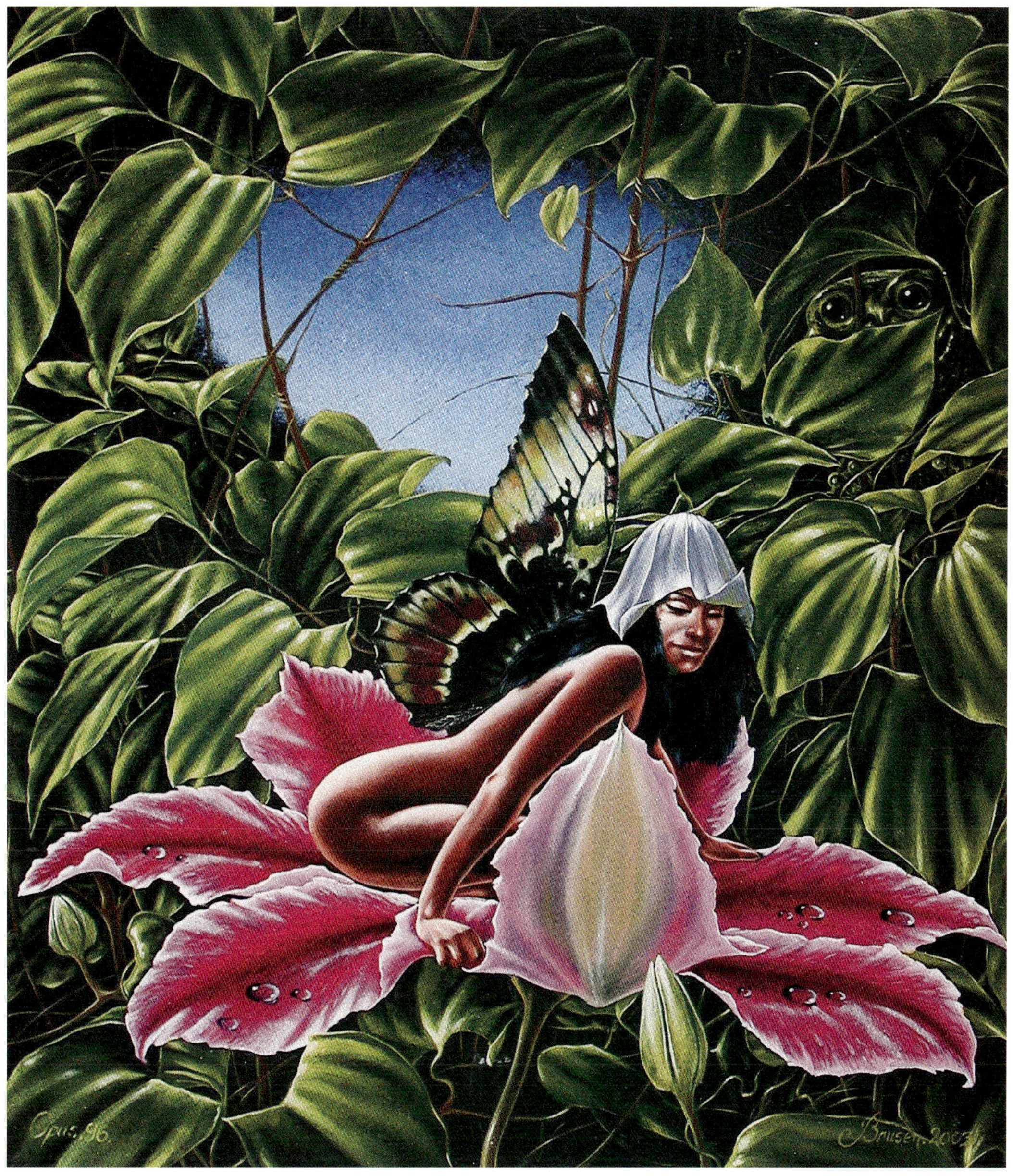

OPUS 97

Old Sad Oak

Oil on Wood • 60 x 40 cm • 2003

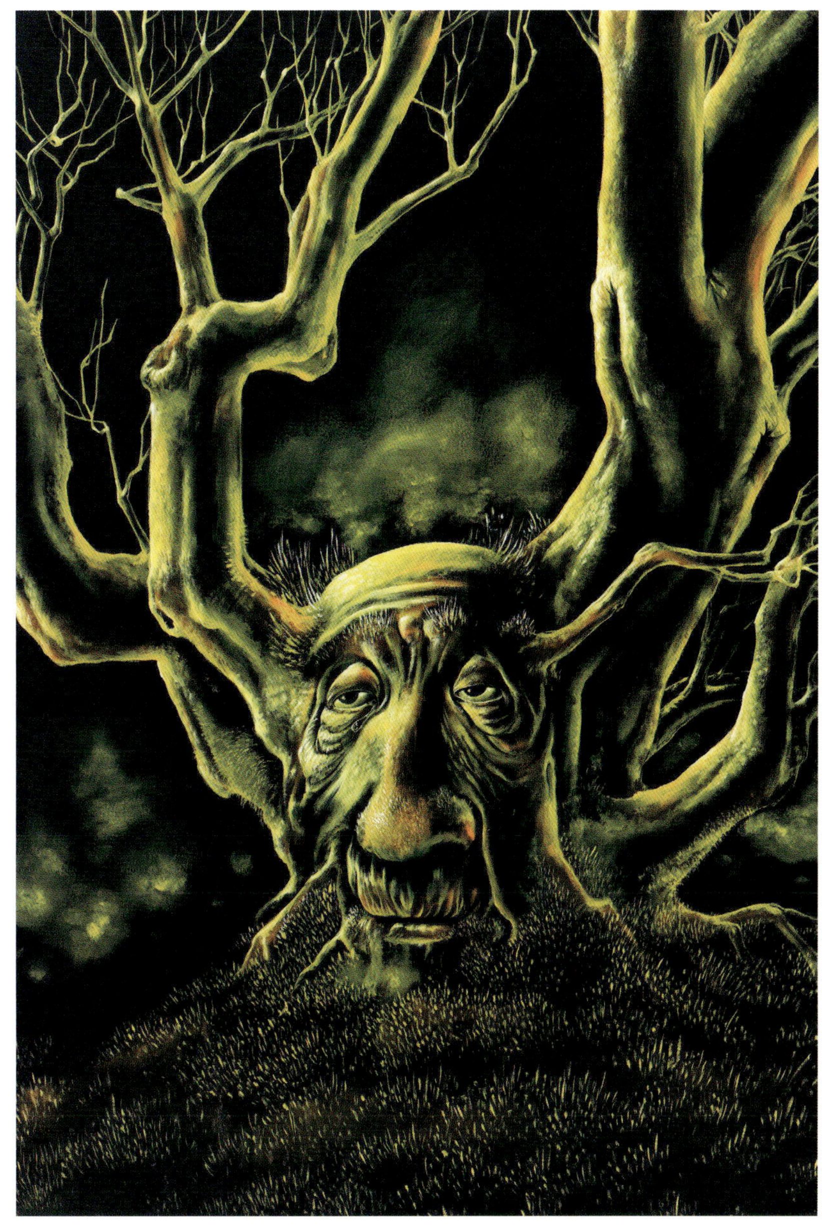

OPUS 98

Mushroom People

Oil on Wood • 30 x 20 cm • 2003

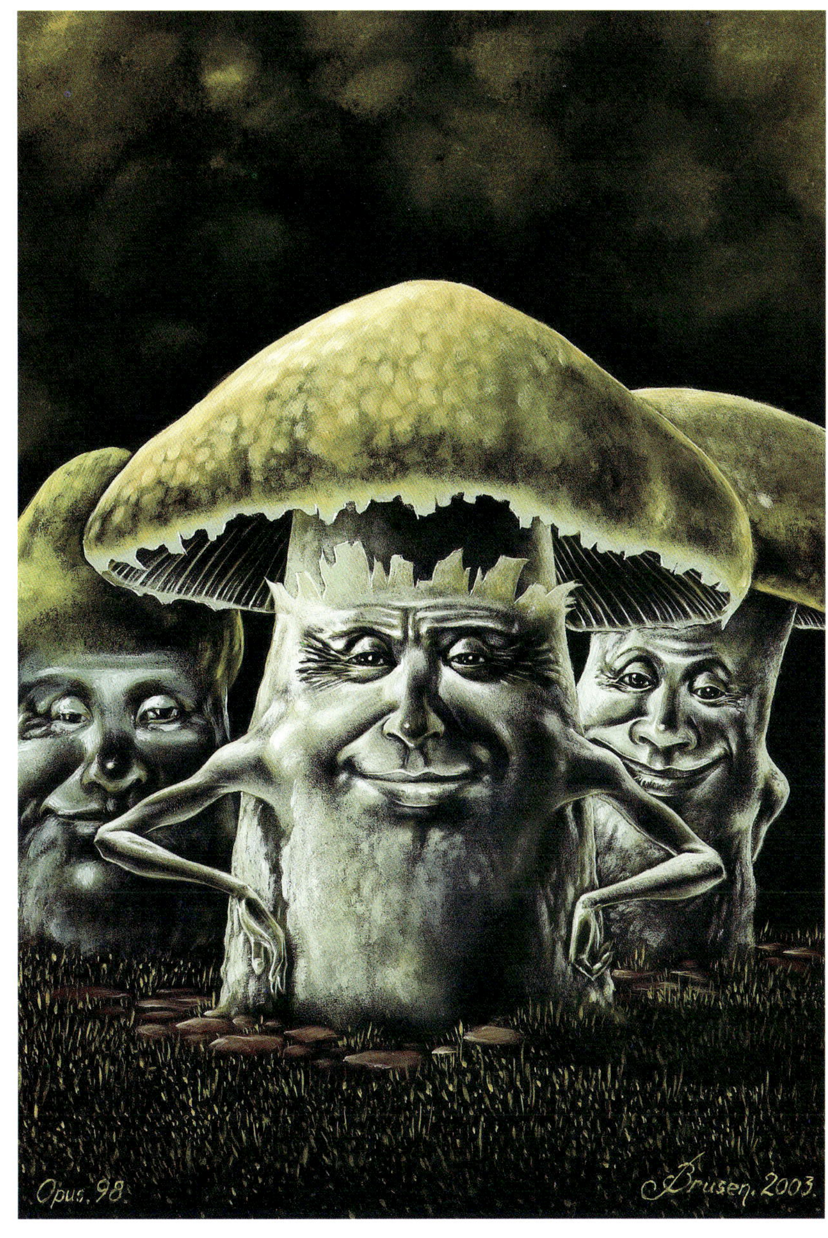
Opus. 98.
Brusen. 2003.

~ OPUS 105 & 106 ~

Mermaid I & II

Both Oil on Wood • 30 x 20 cm • 2003

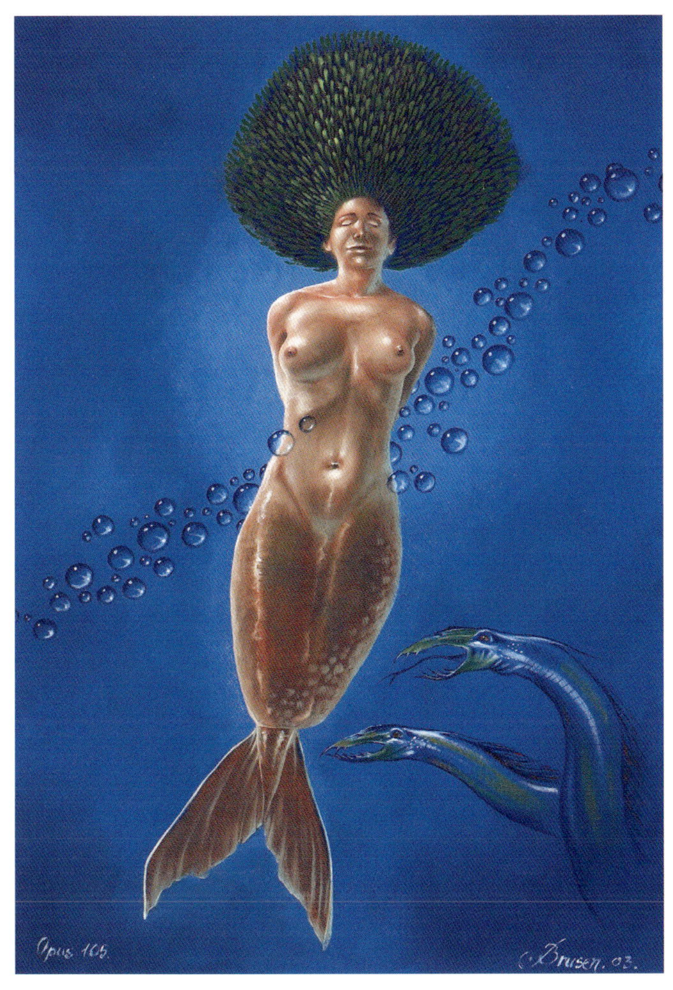
Opus. 105.
Brusen. 03.

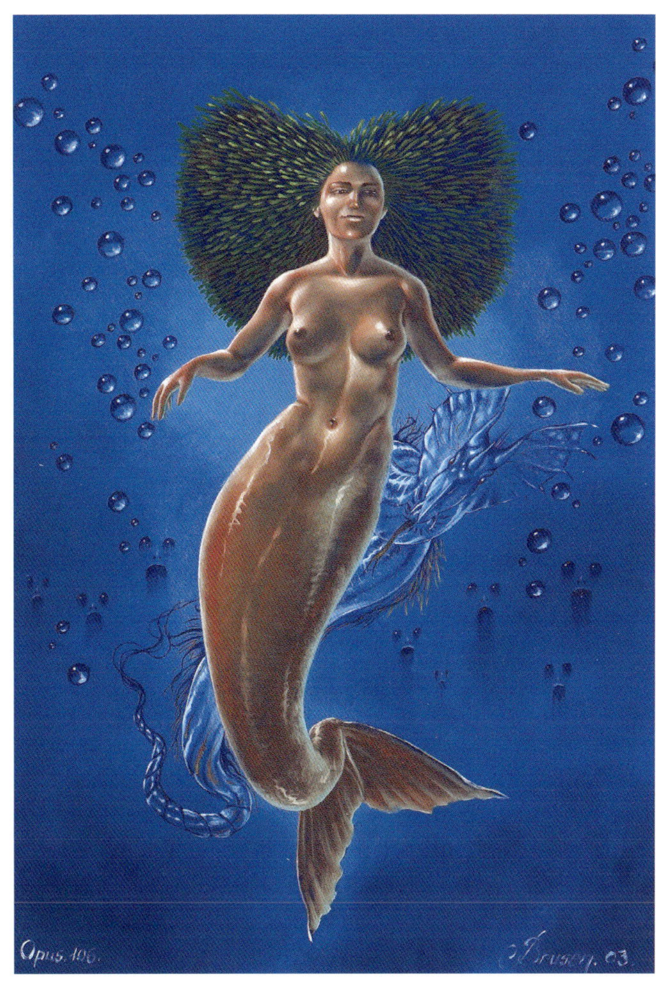
Opus. 106.
Brusen. 03.

OPUS 109

Strawberry Man

Oil on Wood • 18 x 15 cm • 2003

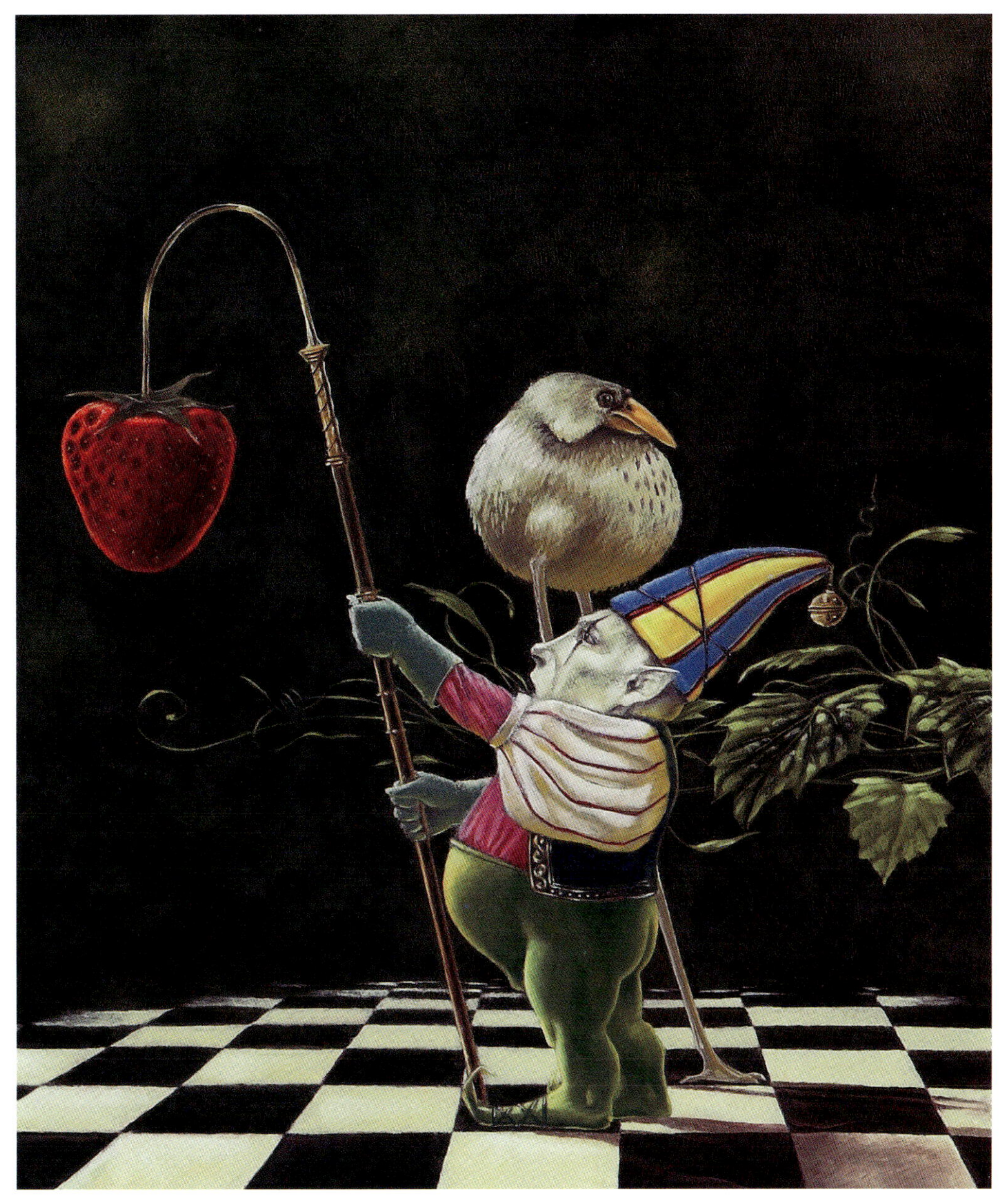

OPUS 111

The Bitch and the Peasant

(Tribute to Carsten Svennson, Danish painter)

Oil on Wood • 20 x 15 cm • 2003

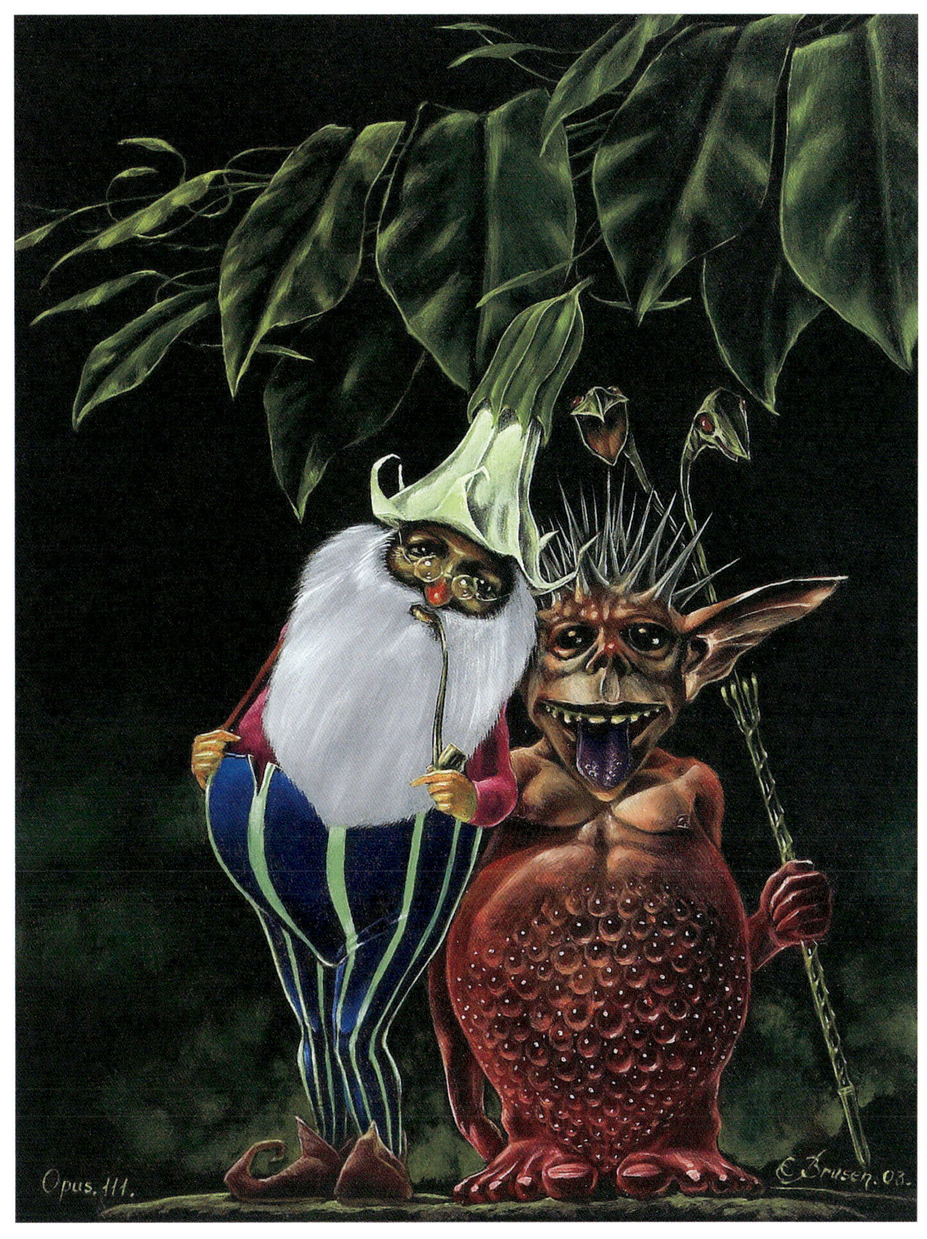
Opus. 111.
E. Brusen. 03.

OPUS 112

The Kiss

Oil on Wood • 20 x 30 cm • 2003

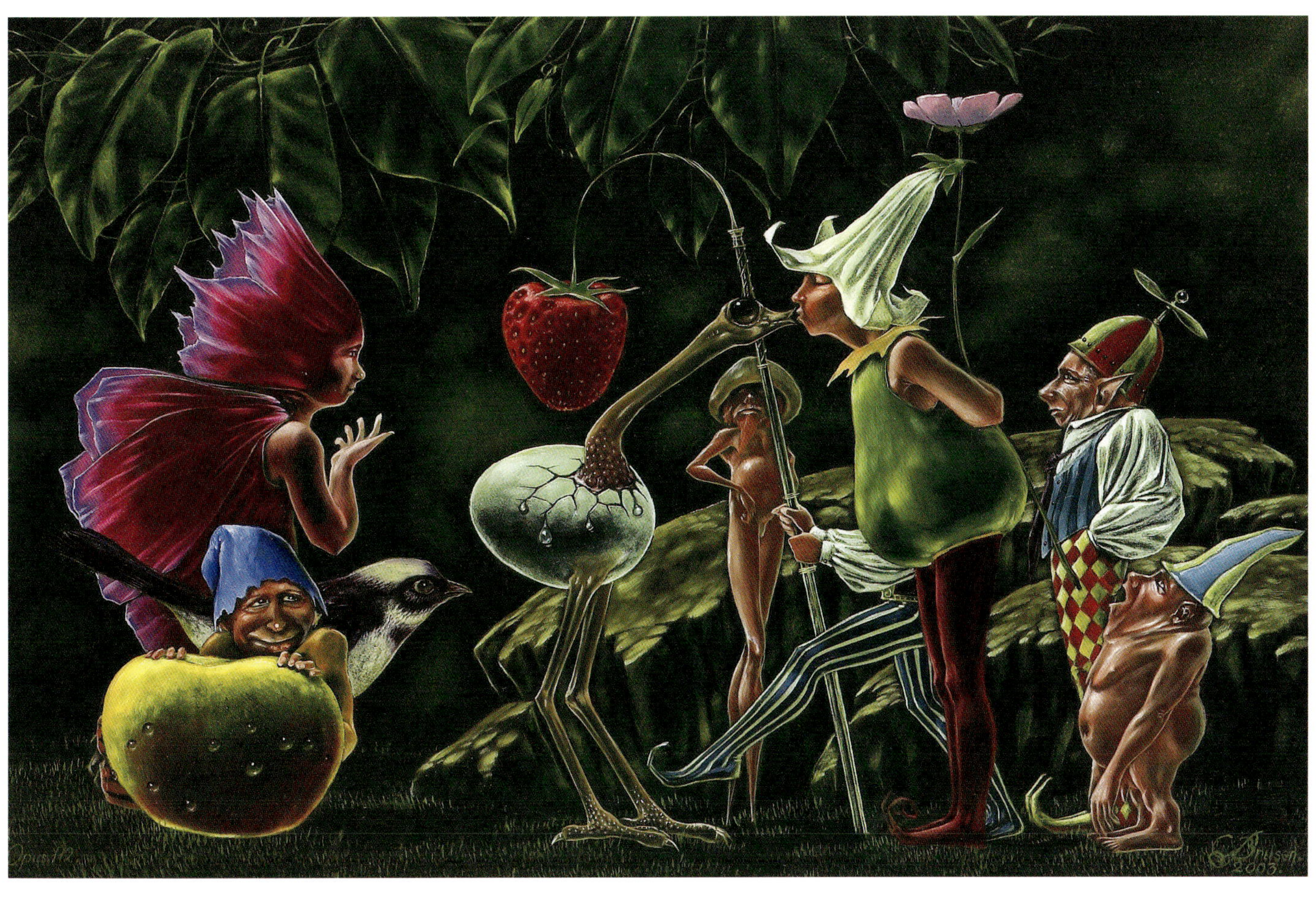

OPUS 114

The Happy Strawberry Collectors

Oil on Wood • 35 x 30 cm • 2003

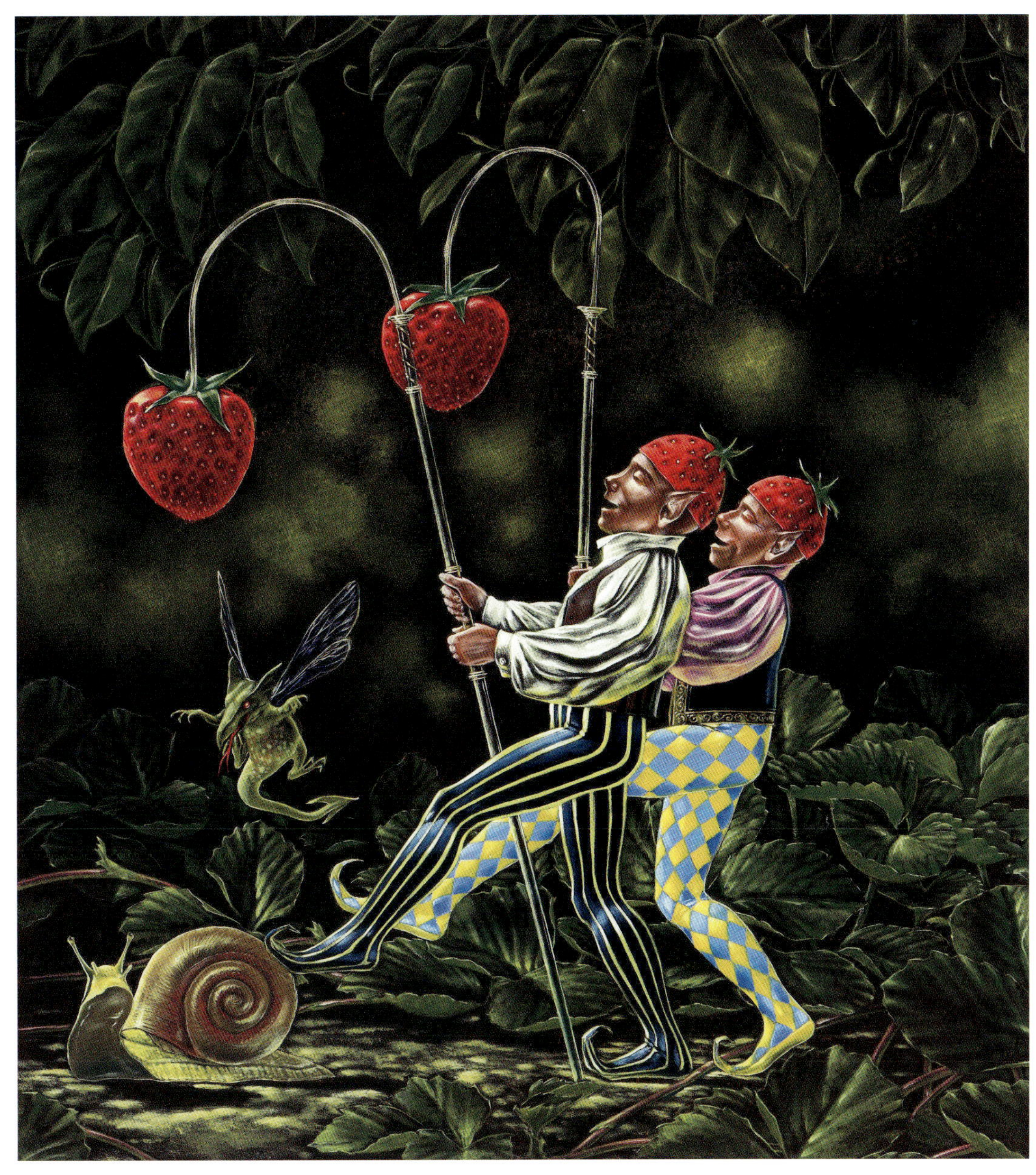

∽ OPUS 116 ∼

And the vote goes to!!!

Oil on Wood • 50 x 40 cm • 2003

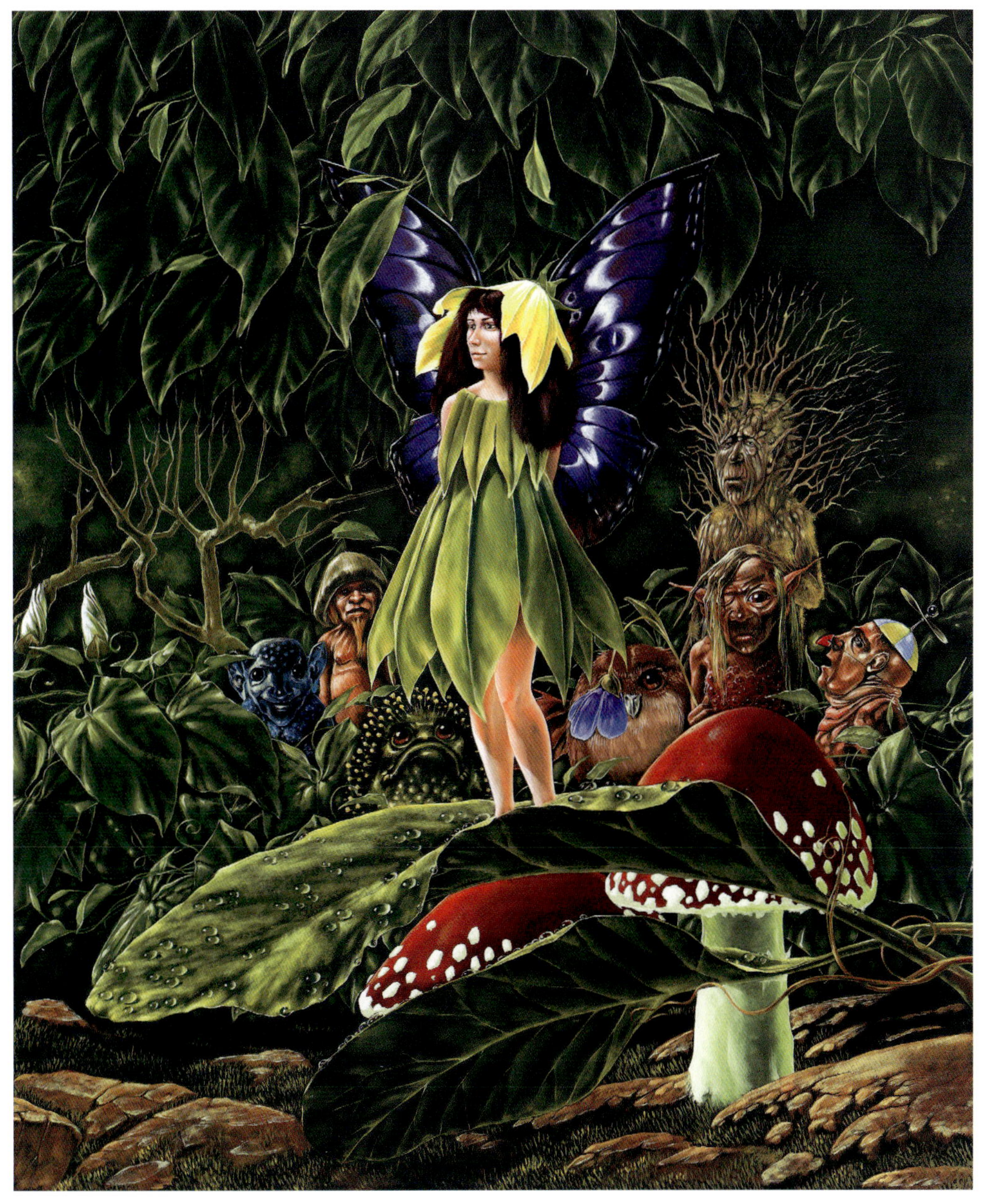

OPUS 122

Campanula Concerto, Opus 122

Oil on Wood • 37 x 48 cm • 2004

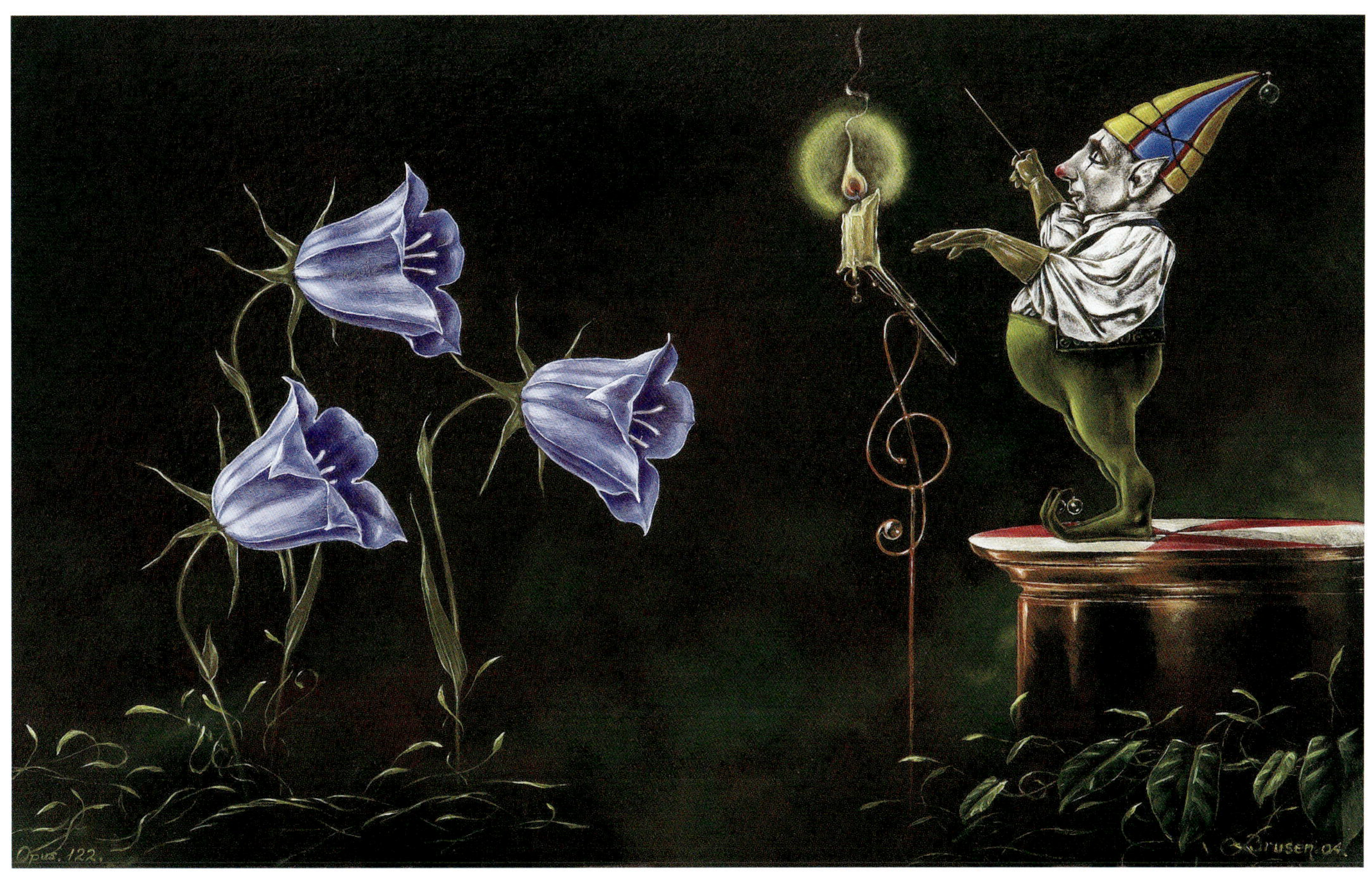
Opus. 122.

OPUS 123

Where is Nactalius

Oil on Wood • 20 x 30 cm • 2004

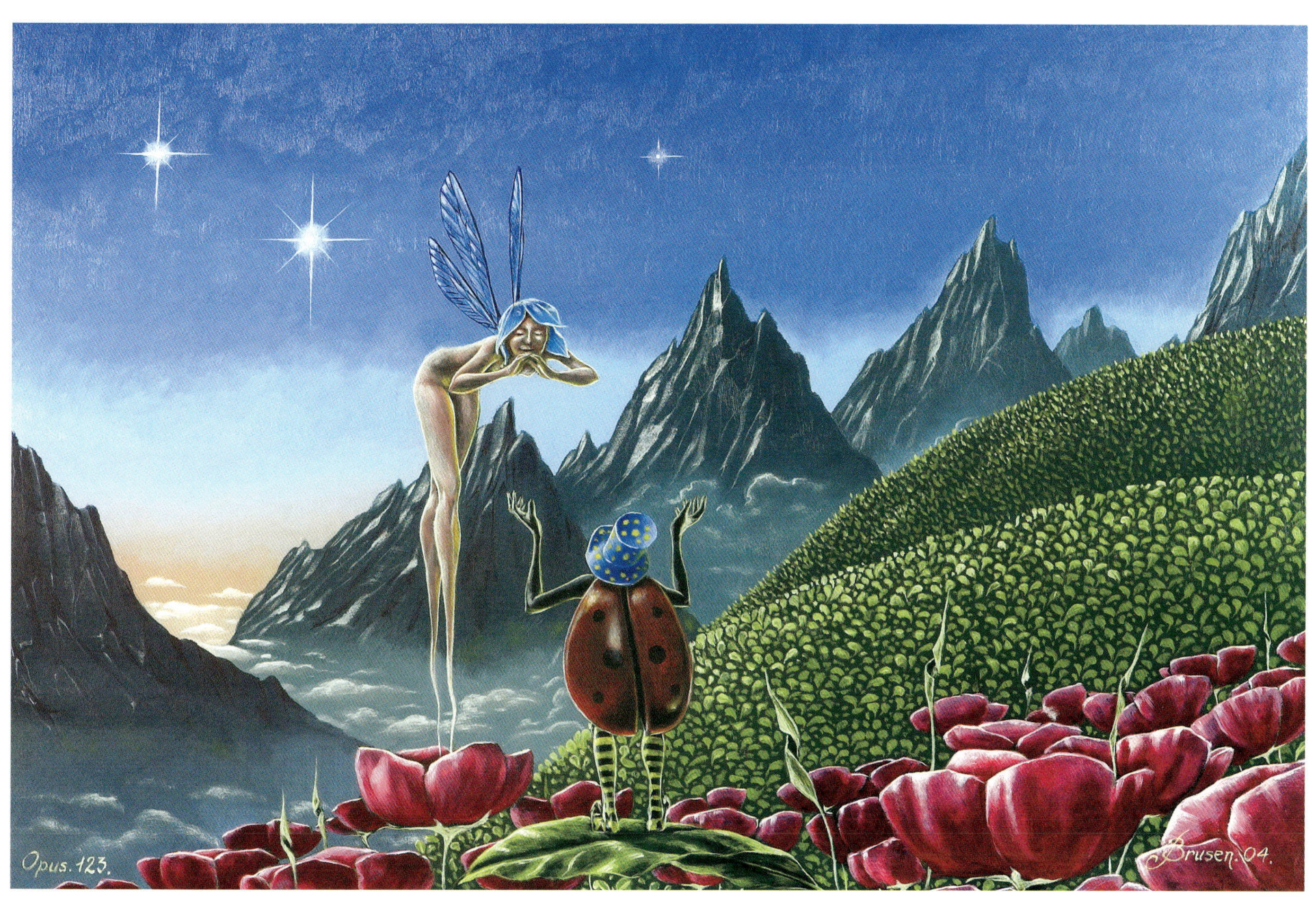
Opus. 123.
Brusen. 04.

OPUS 124

Thee for Two

Oil on Wood • 20 x 15 cm • 2004

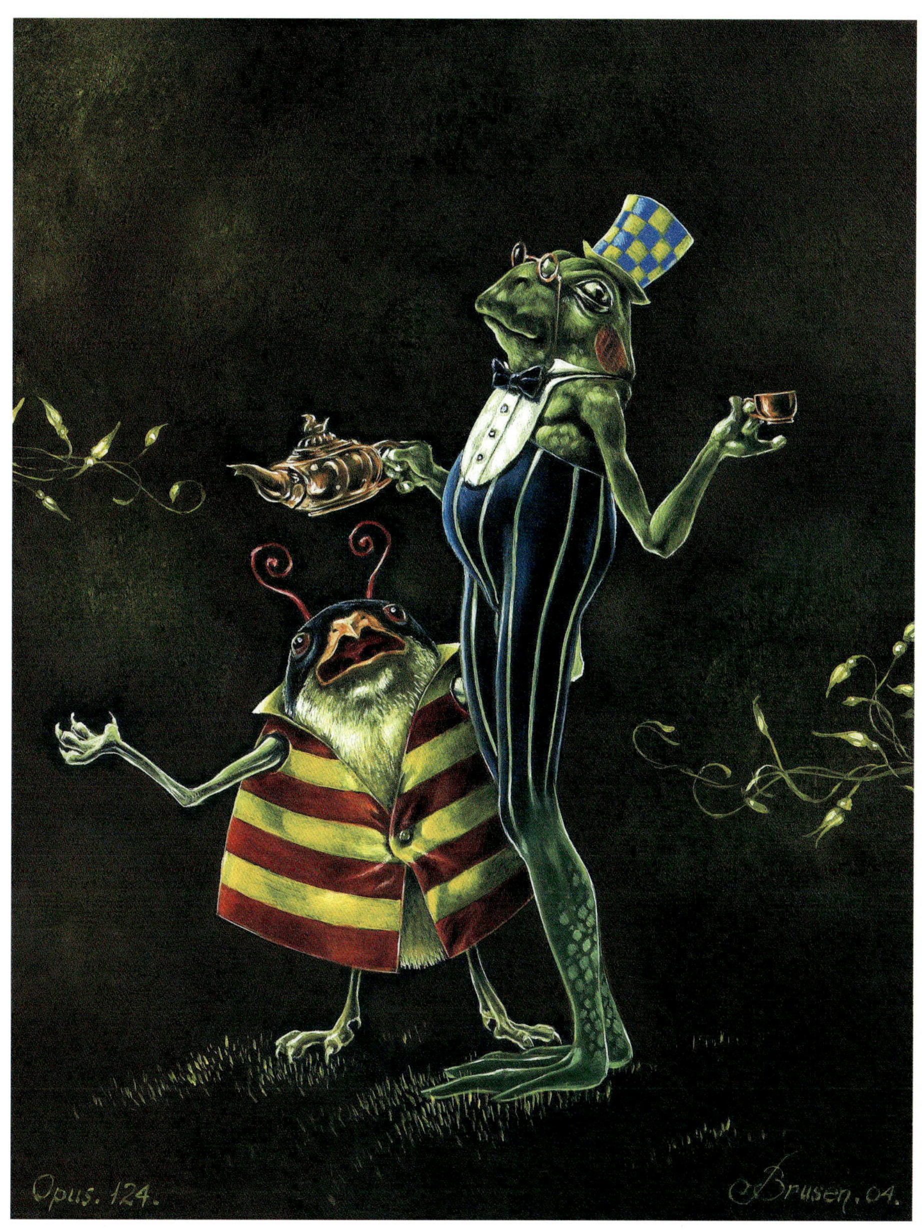
Opus. 124.
Brusen. 04.

OPUS 125

The Excursion (triptych)

Oil on Wood • 45 x 80 cm *including frame* • 2004

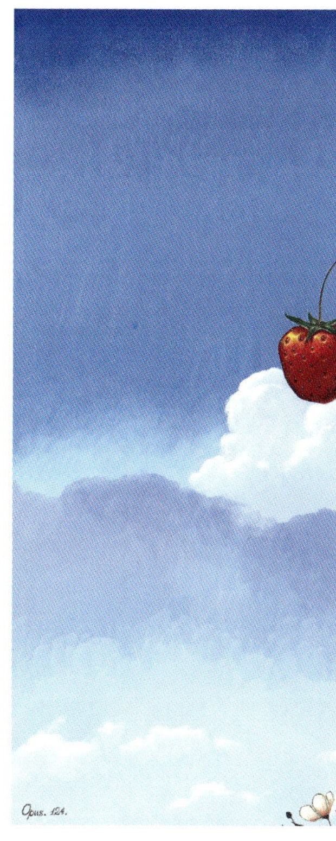
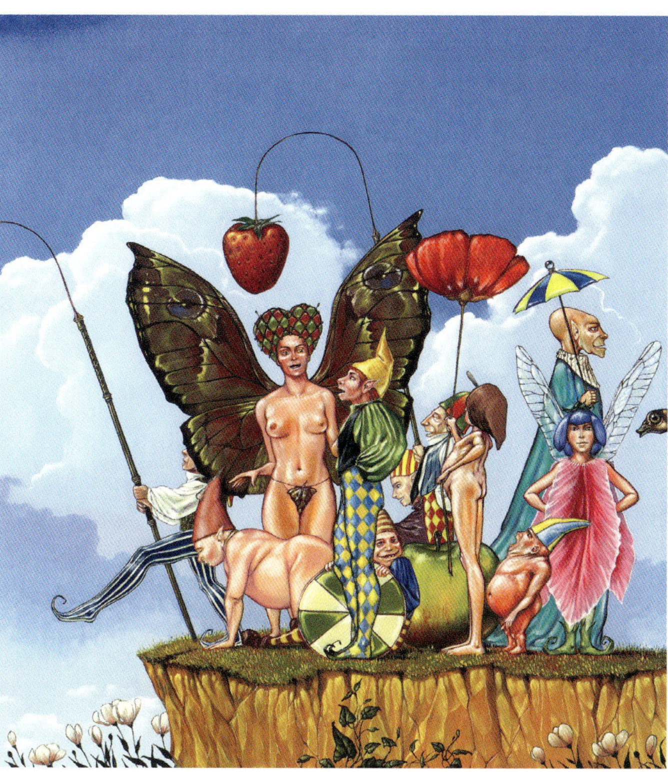
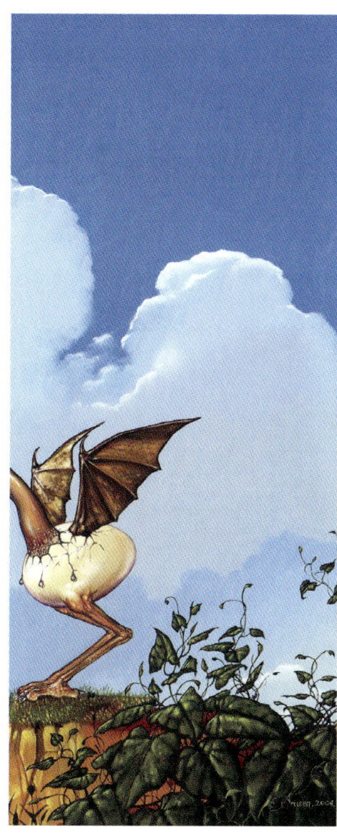

~ OPUS 133 ~

The Nightwatcher

Oil on Wood • 35 x 30 cm • 2004

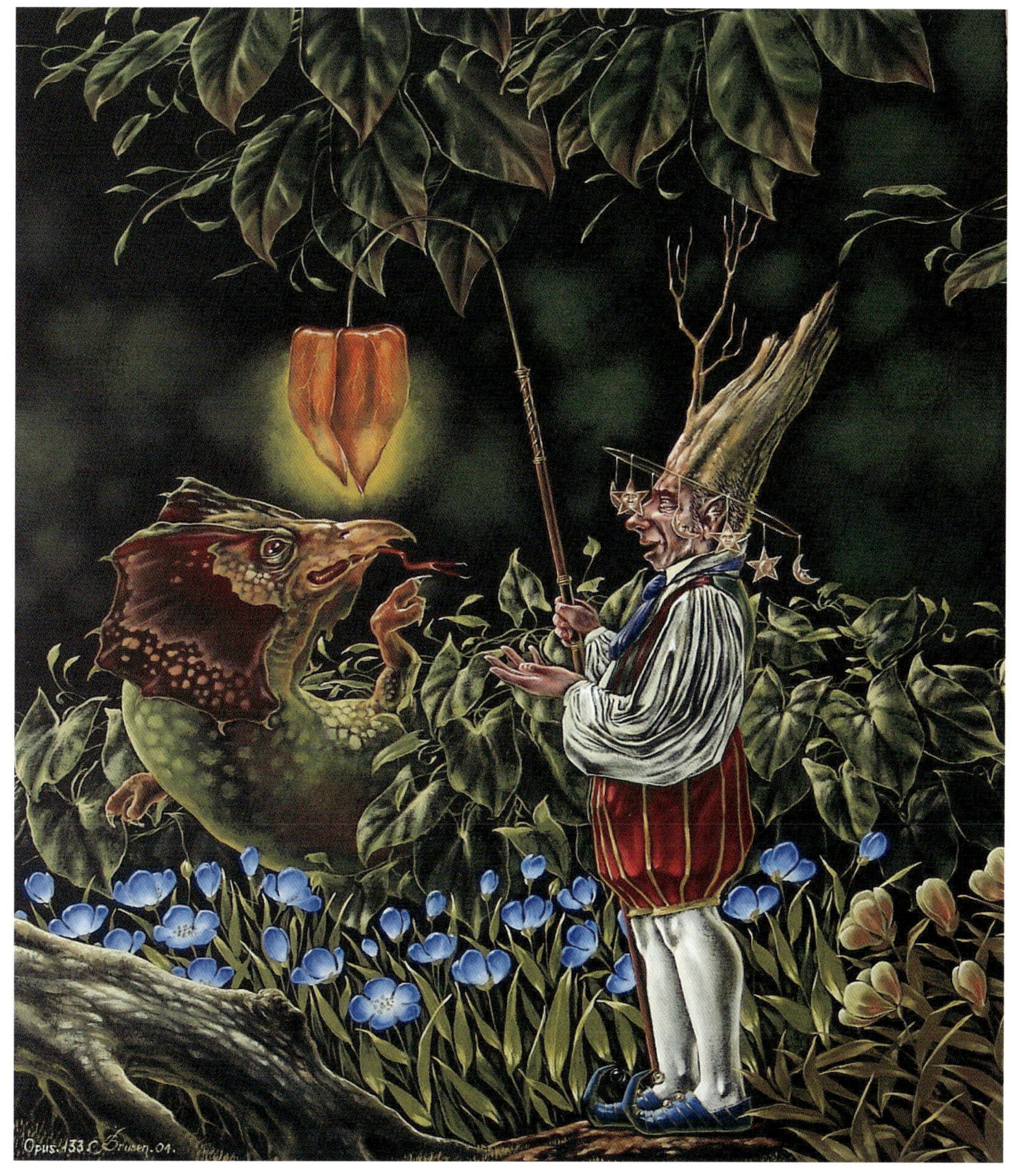
Opus. 133 C. Brusen. 04.

OPUS 134

Ladybird Flying to the Land of Makebelieve

Oil on Wood • 20 x 15 cm • 2004

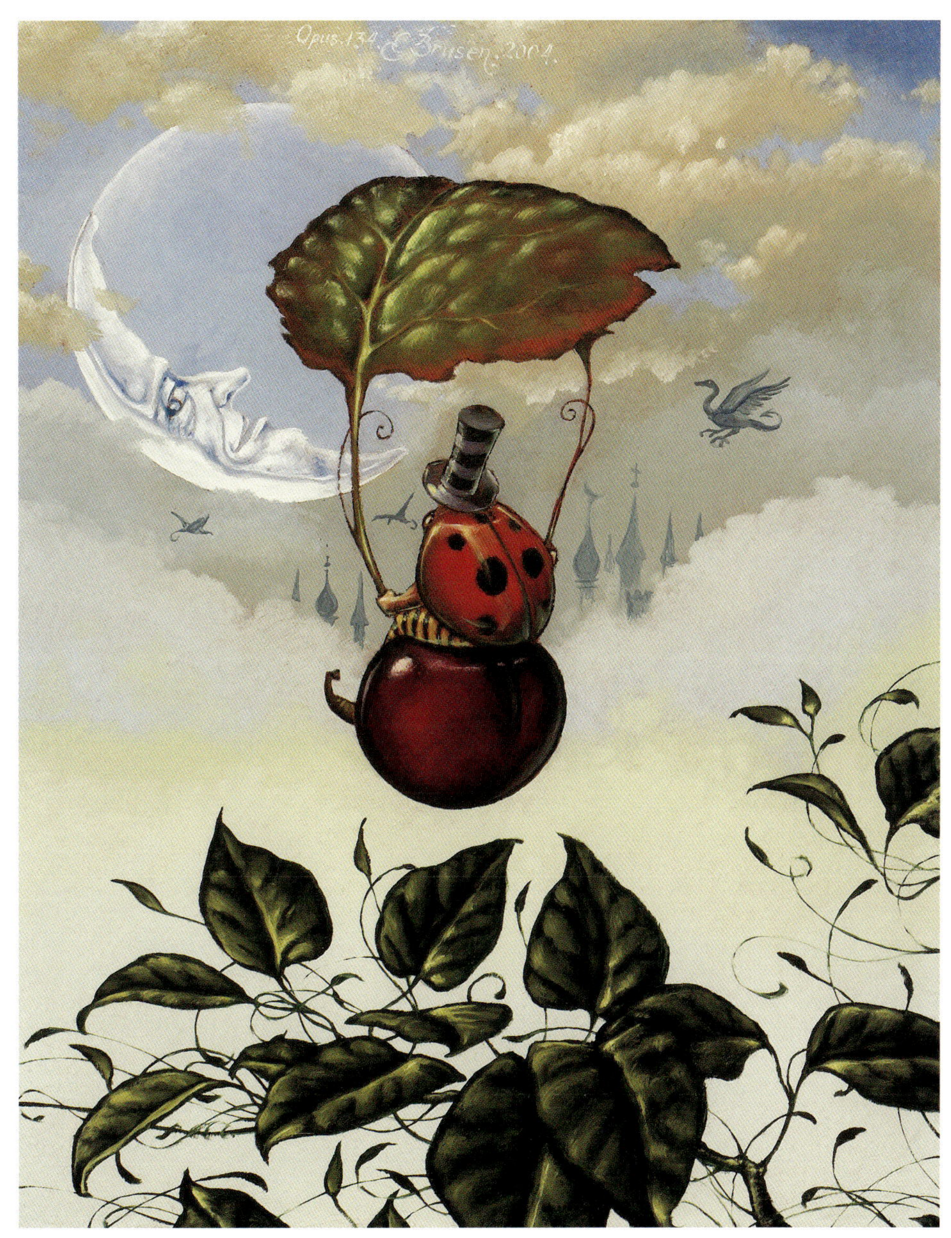

OPUS 136

Moonmadness - Sweet Strawberry

Oil on Wood • 75 x 100 cm • 2005

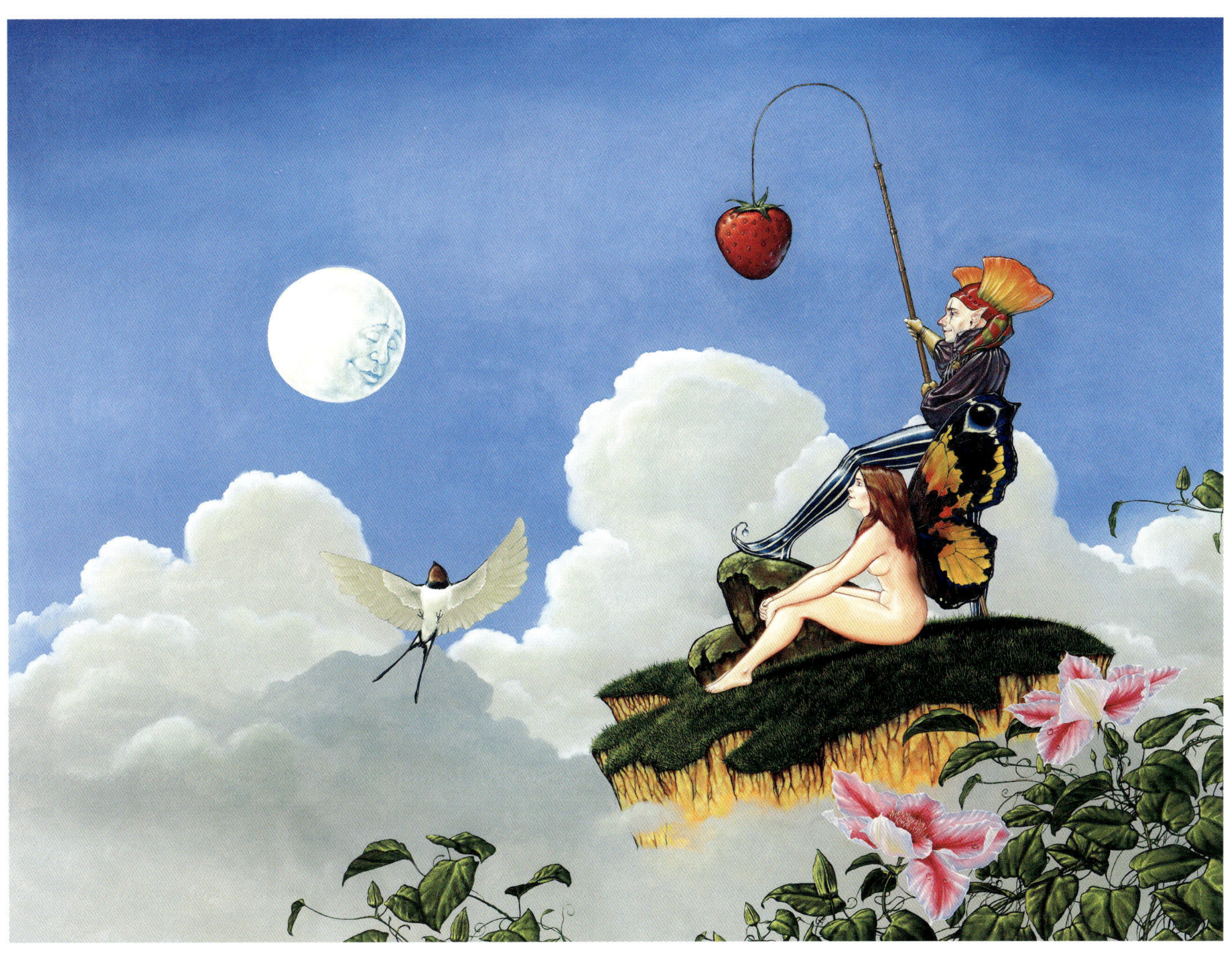

~ OPUS 137 ~

The Happy Parade

Oil on Wood • 80 x 122 cm • 2005

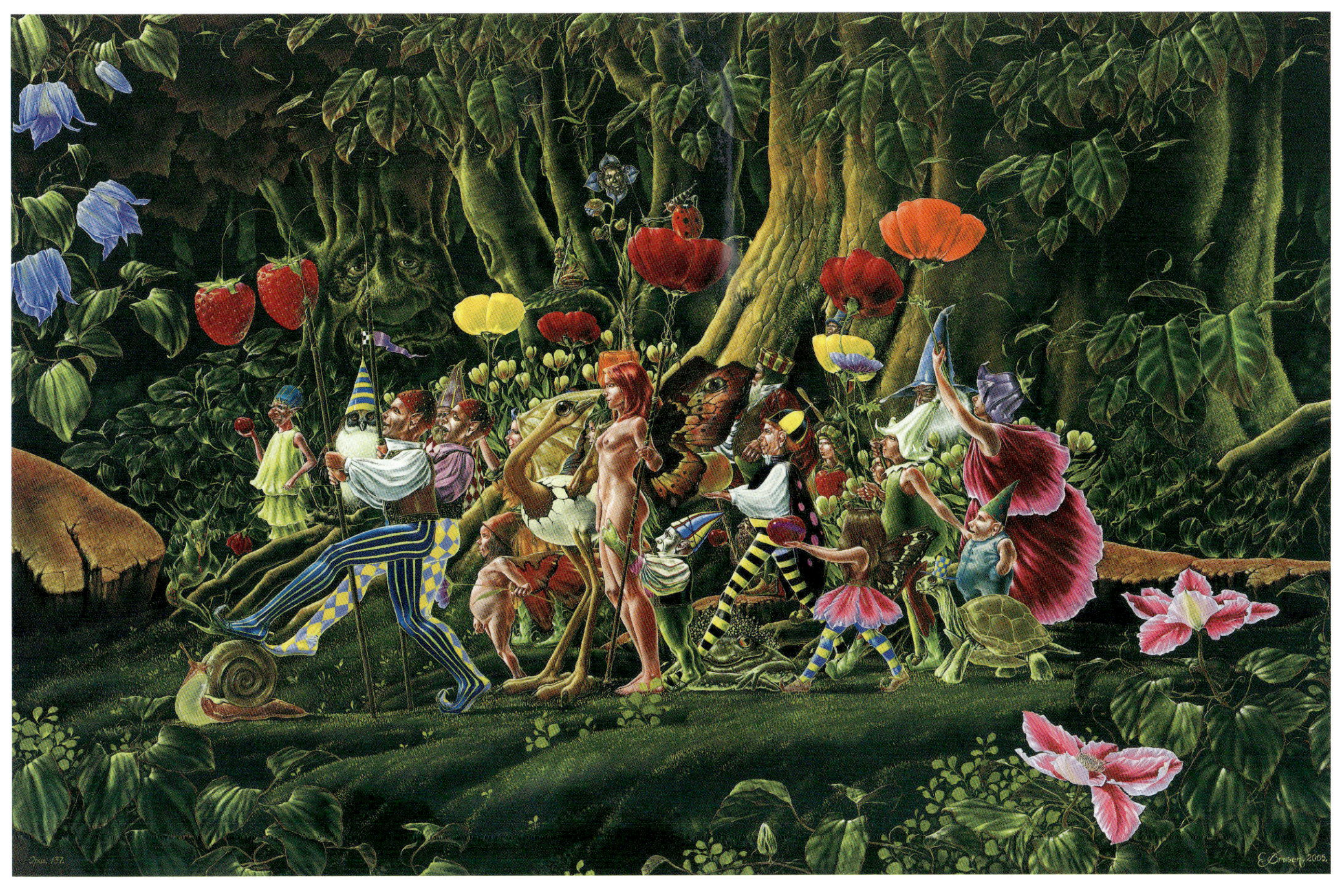

OPUS 138

Cello Concert in Green Minor

Oil on Wood • 49 x 40 cm • 2005

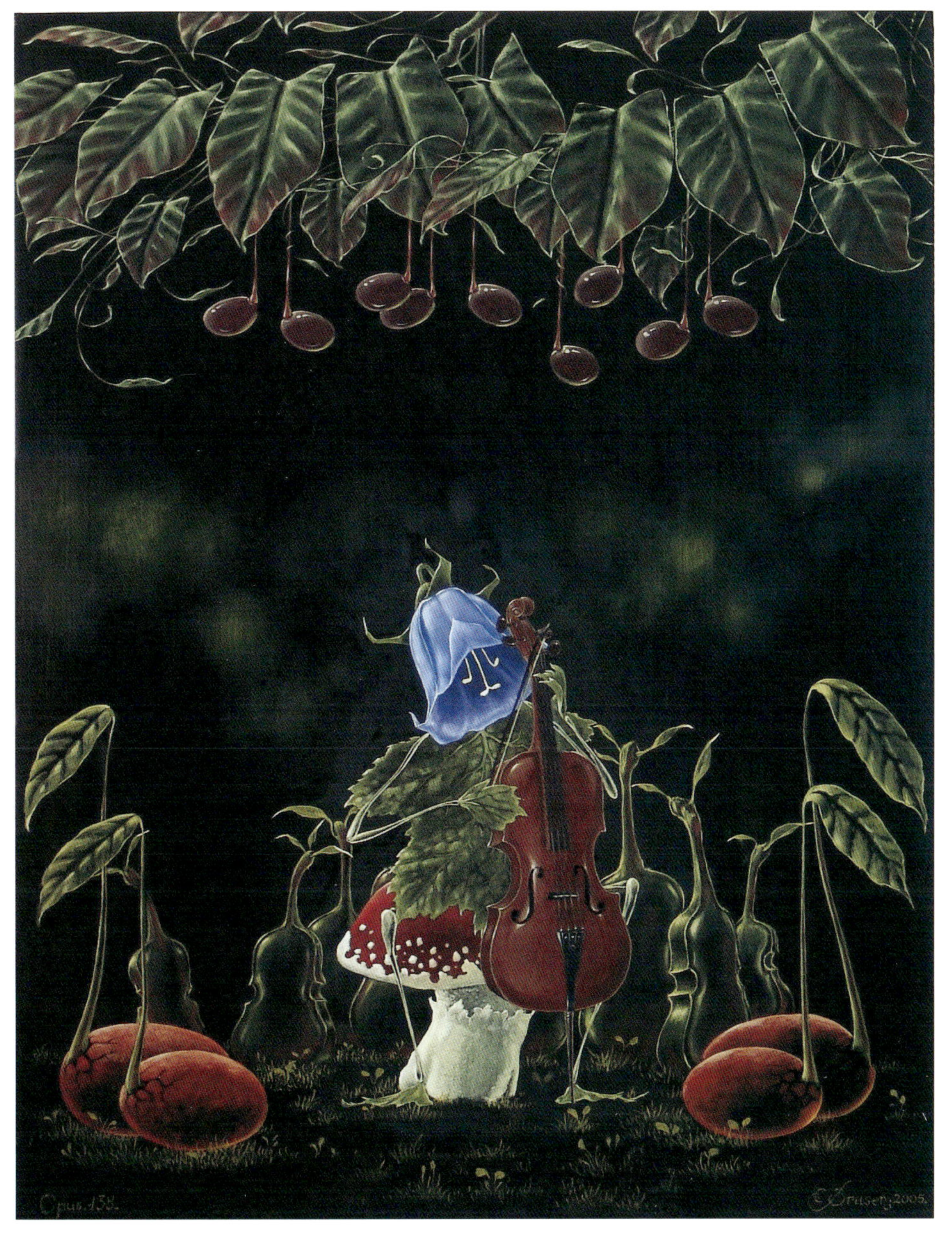

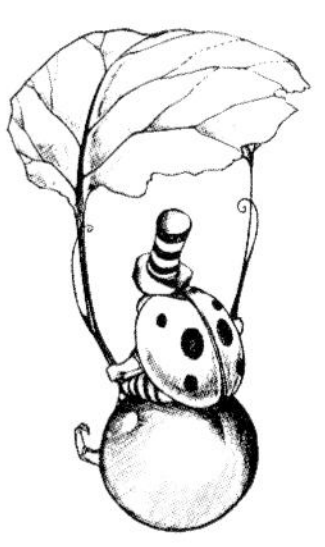

www.clausbrusen.com